O

THE PHILO

COMMUNICATION

Gary P. Radford
Fairleigh Dickinson University

THOMSON
™
WADSWORTH

Australia • Canada • Mexico • Singapore • Spain • United Kingdom • United States

Printer: Thomson West

ISBN 0-534-59574-X

For more information about our products, contact us at:
Thomson Learning Academic Resource Center
1-800-423-0563

For permission to use material from this text or product, submit a request online at
http://www.thomsonrights.com.
Any additional questions about permissions can be submitted by email to
thomsonrights@thomson.com.

Thomson Wadsworth
10 Davis Drive
Belmont, CA 94002-3098
USA

Asia
Thomson Learning
5 Shenton Way #01-01
UIC Building
Singapore 068808

Australia/New Zealand
Thomson Learning
102 Dodds Street
Southbank, Victoria 3006
Australia

Canada
Nelson
1120 Birchmount Road
Toronto, Ontario M1K 5G4
Canada

Europe/Middle East /South Africa
Thomson Learning
High Holborn House
50/51 Bedford Row
London WC1R 4LR
United Kingdom

Latin America
Thomson Learning
Seneca, 53
Colonia Polanco
11560 Mexico D.F.
Mexico

Spain/Portugal
Paraninfo
Calle/Magallanes, 25
28015 Madrid, Spain

Contents

For my mentors

Stanley A. Deetz
Guy Fielding
Patrik Holt
Richard Taylor

and my inspirations

Marie Radford
Meg Radford

Preface

What is communication?

This is the question I ask at the beginning of the every course I teach in my capacity as a teacher of Communication Studies. Invariably I receive the same kinds of answers from my students: "Communication is the transmission of ideas from a source to a receiver," or something very similar. Reflect a moment on the answer you would give to my question "What is communication?" Feel the words form into coherent sentences. Where are those words coming from? Have you ever wondered why it is you are forming your answer in these specific terms and not others? Have you ever wondered what a different answer to this question would look like? Or if a different kind of answer is even possible?

It might be said that this book is not about communication at all. It is more about *you*, the reader, and the *experience* of how you are able to articulate an understanding of the term "communication." You may have different reasons for needing to articulate such an understanding. You may be an undergraduate student, approaching the study of communication for the first time. You may be an advanced undergraduate or a graduate student looking to extend your knowledge of communication into areas beyond the traditional "source sends message to receiver" perspectives. You may be a lay reader who has picked this book from the shelf at Barnes and Noble and find yourself intrigued at the question "What is communication?" This book is intended for anyone who is interested in communication, both as an academic subject and as an area of general interest, since all of us give very similar answers. The questions I want to address are: "Why do we produce such consistently similar answers?" and "How might we articulate different answers?"

The book does not follow what might be considered an orthodox structure or a predictable line on the subject of communication. I have attempted to incorporate a diverse range of voices that resonate throughout the responses of my students. These voices include those of Claude Shannon and Warren Weaver, a standard for all who are interested in contemporary ways of talking about communication. However, I have also included less predictable voices, such as those of empiricist philosopher John Locke, the pioneering experimental psychologist Wilhelm Wundt, the novelist George Orwell, the phenomenologist Edmund Husserl, and the literary and art historian Hans-Georg Gadamer, among others. This book is not a review of a series of communication theories. Nor is it a history of the communication concept throughout the ages. It is an examination of how and why we talk about communication the way we do. As the book progresses, it is also an examination of how we might transcend these ways of speaking.

There are many people to thank in making this book a reality. Daniel Kolak, editor of the Wadsworth Philosophical Topics Series, has been an incredible inspiration and mentor to me. My wife and intellectual partner, Marie L. Radford, has provided unfailing technical and emotional support. She commented on many drafts of these chapters, proofread the final manuscript many times, and prepared the index. Harriet Selverstone proofread and copyedited the final manuscript. Dr. Jonathan Taylor made this book possible by reviving my aching and ailing back caused by many, many hours of sitting in front of my computer. Keith Abramson, a senior in Communication Studies, and Lucretia Koba, a graduate student in the MA program in Corporate and Organizational Communication, both at Fairleigh Dickinson University, gave me invaluable feedback and should consider themselves Model Readers of this text. I would also like to acknowledge the Becton College of Arts and Sciences at Fairleigh Dickinson University for supporting the writing of this book through an Assigned Release Time for Research Award. Thanks also to all of my colleagues in the Department of English, Communication, and Philosophy at Fairleigh Dickinson University for their unwavering enthusiasm and encouragement of this work, especially my Department Chair, Dr. Geoffrey Weinman. My parents, Howard and Elsie Radford, provided the constant love and support throughout my life that has enabled me to achieve whatever potential I might have. My daughter, Meg Radford, fulfills her role as "light of my life" with unconditional warmth and love and is always willing to remind me that I am "the best Dad." She is the best mentor of all. Finally, thank you to Richard Taylor, my English and Drama teacher at Sutton Centre Comprehensive School, who quite literally forced me to read George Orwell's *1984* when I was eleven years old. The reason, he told me, was that even I could write better stories than the James Bond novels I was reading at the time. Mr. Taylor's determination to have me read "good literature" set me on a path that has led to this book appearing today and I dedicate chapter six, "Which Do You Wish?," especially to him.

Gary P. Radford

One

How We Talk About Communication Today: *The Regime of Communication*

If you were to ask the first ten people you meet on the street to define "communication," all ten would likely give some version of what we call the transmission theory. (W. Barnett Pearce)

Barnett Pearce's observation that "if you were to ask the first ten people on the street to define 'communication,' all ten would likely give some version of what we call the transmission theory" reflects my own experience in discussing the nature of communication with students, academics, and lay people. I actually found Pearce's observation to be quite comforting. It confirmed for me a feeling I have had for many years: that most people have a firm and quite unproblematic notion of communication.

I speak as an associate professor of a discipline referred to as Communication Studies. I have both studied and taught the subject since 1980, some 24 years at the time I am writing this book. In just about every course I have taught, whether it be an undergraduate-level "Introduction to Communication" course, an upper-level course in communication theory, or a graduate-level course in corporate communication, I ask this question:

1

What is communication?

A simple question, but an important one. After all, these students are gaining degrees in communication. They really should know what is meant by the term. Like Barnett Pearce, I have found that the answers all these students give me are extremely consistent and, in their view, totally unproblematic. After all, it's obvious; communication is a process of transmission: "Communication is the exchange of ideas," they say. "It's the process by which a message is transmitted to another person. It's about making oneself understood."

All students nod in agreement, secure in their consensus. Some students throw in terms they have come across in other communication classes, such as "sender," "receiver," "encode," and "decode." But it all comes down to the same basic idea: communication is about a message moving from one place to another and, at this level, it all seems very straightforward.

"I have an idea," they elaborate, "and I transmit it to you, and you have the idea. If the ideas are the same, we have communicated."

The transmission view of communication, in a nutshell.

I often ask the students that since they know so much about communication already, why do they need to take a course in the subject or even, for that matter, a whole degree program. Again, the students come up with familiar and very consistent answers.

"We want to know how to communicate better," they say.

"Why do you wish to communicate better?" I ask.

"Having good communication skills will be to our advantage," is the standard line. "Good communicators make their thoughts and intentions clear to others. Good communication is required for high-level jobs where the management of others is crucial. Good communication will help me live a more successful social and family life. Taking a communication course will provide a gateway into a communication career in television, radio, journalism, advertising, or public relations."

For many communication students, this is what the study of communication is all about: to become skilled with a set of tools and strategies which they can use to further themselves in their lives and careers. When I ask students what it means to be "skilled," they reply that an intended receiver or audience will have the idea they want them to have, perform the behavior they want them to perform, or have the attitude they wish them to hold. Hickson and Stacks (1993) agree that students in communication classes are most interested in pragmatic outcomes. They write that students "want to know why certain communication strategies provide the best results, how to obtain the best possible communication outcome, and in general how to predict how their and others' communication will be received. In sum, students want to understand and predict communicative acts" (p. 261). What is very clear to me after many years of having these discussions is that what is problematic about communication is not what it "is," that much seems to be obvious, but rather how successfully one can exploit it.

There is nothing unusual in the responses that students give to me. Indeed, I would be amazed if they said anything different. Communication scholar James Carey (1992) argues that the transmission view is the most prevalent conception of communication in our culture, and perhaps in all industrialized cultures. Carey writes:

> Our basic orientation to communication remains grounded, at the deepest roots of our thinking, in the idea of transmission: communication is a process whereby messages are transmitted and distributed in space for the control of distance and people. (p. 15)

Michael Reddy (1979) claims that the transmission view provides the fundamental semantic structures of the stories English speakers tell about communication. When talking about communication, people have no choice but to conform to a culturally prescribed grammar embedded in these typical expressions concerning communication:

- "Try to get your thoughts across more clearly."
- "Stan communicated his ideas very clearly."
- "I need to get my ideas across."

Rare is the student who enquires as to the nature of communication as opposed to the manner in which it might be used or exploited. So I diligently move on to ask the students not to describe what communication can do, but to describe for me what this thing called communication is that can lead to all these wonderful outcomes. This, again, generates a consistent set of unproblematic responses to begin with. However, the discussion becomes much more frustrating the longer we go.

The Idea of the Idea

For many students, the beginning of the communication process begins with the sender, and with an idea the sender wishes to convey to a receiver.

"I have a thought in my head," they say, "and I want to let you know what it is."

So far, so good. Then I ask the question that brings down the complete house of cards.

"OK," I say, "communication begins with the idea or the thought to be communicated, yes? Can you tell me what you mean by 'idea'? What is the nature of this 'idea' that it is the purpose of communication to transmit?"

With one question, we are immediately thrust into the labyrinth of questions and issues that have plagued philosophers of the likes of Descartes, Locke, Hume, and Kant:

- What is an idea?
- What is knowledge?
- How can I know what is in your mind?
- How can I know what is around me?
- How can my mind represent what is around me?
- How does an idea relate to the world?

Up until this question, the notion that communication was a process of moving ideas around was unproblematic. With the asking of the question "What is an idea?," it becomes an absolute morass. Like Descartes, Locke, Hume, and all the great minds before them, the students struggle to come up with a coherent and easy answer.

"Well, ideas exist in the brain," they say, "and these ideas are encoded into symbols, and the symbols are transmitted to another person, that person receives the symbols, their brain decodes the symbols, and interprets the ideas the sender intended to send."

So I say: "Is what you have described 'real' or just a story you have told me to get me off your back?" And further, "how would you know the difference?"

Students typically begin by arguing this is real. After all, isn't this common sense?

"Ideas are real, aren't they? We all have ideas."

So, I ask again, "What is an idea?"

Now we are really stuck.

"Well, it's something in my head."

"And what form does it take in your head?"

4

At this point, students are forced to resort to some unfamiliar language concerning electrical and chemical processes. They try to piece together an explanation using terms such as "synapses," "neurons," or even "neural networks." They scramble to retrieve and articulate terms they learned in their "Introduction to Psychology" class.

"And what do you know about these processes?"

Not much, if anything.

"So why are you telling me this? Where did you hear this stuff?"

The usual response is that these are words they have heard elsewhere; fragments of explanations they have heard on the Discovery Channel or from a psychology class long forgotten. They are not quite sure how it all works exactly, but they feel comfortable in the knowledge that they at least have some words that provide some degree of comfort.

"Can you experience these processes?" I ask. "Can you feel these chemical and electric processes happening in your head?"

"No."

"Have you ever seen a human brain?"

"No."

"If you did, do you think you could see these processes happening? Could you see ideas being formed and being moved around?"

"No."

"Then on what evidence are you telling me this? On what basis can you tell me that communication involves 'the exchange of ideas' when you don't know what an idea is in any tangible form?"

The students usually rebel at this point. The discussion has reached a dead end. We have reached the limits of the language available to them to explain this apparently simple and unproblematic notion: the fact we have ideas. What slowly becomes apparent is that their previously unproblematic understanding of communication is founded on a concept of "idea" that is totally problematic, unknowable, and ultimately incomprehensible to them. I point out to them that the philosopher Ludwig Wittgenstein would refer to this whole discourse as "disguised nonsense" (Wittgenstein, 1953, p. 133e). Their discourse gives the impression that their words actually refer to something tangible, that they have a "sense," when in fact the whole exercise we have just engaged in was a language game. I ask questions about communication, the students give me answers using some appropriate vocabulary that they think will satisfy the demands of the question.

As my questions move beyond familiar linguistic terrain, the students fall back into unfamiliar discourses and begin using terms such as "synapses," "neurons," and "brain functions." It is not that the students express a deeper knowledge by invoking such language. Rather, they move from one discursive system to another as their language in one domain runs out. Why did the students begin introducing terms such as "neuron" and "synapse" in their explanation of what an idea was? Because they know something about neurophysiology? Not really. Their goal was to fashion a statement that would satisfy the demands of the discussion. Eventually, their linguistic resources run out altogether, and this is the point at which they accuse me of playing games with their minds. I am quick to remind them I am not playing games with their minds at all. I am playing games with their language. I am attempting to make them aware of the linguistic resources they seek and employ in order to continue this conversation.

I suppose the students could have simply said "I don't know," but this is very rare and is not considered an acceptable response in a language game between student and teacher. Students will typically keep using language until they have run out of moves to make. The students express their frustration by targeting it at me and the perception that my questions are part of some sadistic game rather than something real. But rarely, if ever, is any student prepared to transgress the boundaries of this particular language game. Indeed, despite their frustration, the students prefer to remain within its boundaries. After all this talk is over, ideas and communication will continue to exist in the way I know them, right?

The Regime of Communication

My students' plight, and their reaction to it, remind me of the character of Leonard Shelby in Christopher Nolan's movie *Memento* (Nolan, 1999). Leonard is a man who, following an attack on him and his wife, has no short-term memory and, as a result, has a very limited capacity to make sense of what is going on around him. Leonard constantly reflects on his capacity to make sense of things. At the end of the movie, Leonard states:

> I have to believe in the world outside my own mind. I have to believe that my actions still have meaning, even if I can't remember them. I have to believe that when my eyes are closed, the world's still there (Nolan, 1999).

My students, even if it is for only a brief moment, experience a similar feeling. Through our discussion, they are forced to confront the fact that they cannot explain what is, on the surface, the most mundane of facts: the having of ideas and the expression of those ideas to others. Though the discussion may cause them to close their eyes for a moment and remove the world from view, they are quick to snap back to their prior beliefs that their ideas are still there and communication still exists in the manner they think it does. Like Leonard, they *have to believe* this because what would be the alternative? No world? No ideas? No communication? When the discussion and the class ends, the world (and communication) quickly comes back into focus again. The transmission view of communication regains its version of reality for them.

If nothing else, I use these discussions with my students to instill in them the feeling that perhaps not is all as it seems with respect to communication. What are these feelings of uncertainty and discontent that Radford arouses in me? Why don't my views hold together when asked the most simplistic and obvious of questions such as "What is an idea?" and "How does the mind interpret information?" Cultural studies scholar Lawrence Grossberg (1997) articulates this feeling of uneasiness as follows:

> I have always been deeply suspicious of the concept of communication and the enormous power it has in both academic and popular discourses. I have never been comfortable with its ubiquity; its intentional vagueness, which allowed it to impose an apparent unity on radically diverse practices; its inherent circularity, grounded in a largely unexplored set of philosophical assumptions. (p. 27)

Grossberg (1997) argues that the responses of my students indicate "that we were living in an organization of discursive and ideological power that could be described as 'the regime of communication'" (p. 27). Grossberg's "regime of communication" is a description of how we are forced into certain ways of talking about communication, and the limits that this way of talking imposes on us. During our discussions of communication, I find I can usually make students realize that their statements are the end result of their attempts to formulate acceptable answers to my questions as opposed to some objective description of some real and objective process. Yet, even here, my overpowering sense is that the students remain well and truly trapped in the reality created by this way of talking. It has a tremendous hold over them. Like Grossberg (1997), I found myself "amazed by how often an appeal to the concept of communication was assumed to solve all sorts of theoretical . . . problems" (p. 27). To challenge the transmission view of communication was to challenge reality itself. This challenging often results in quite emotional reactions and outright cynicism as the students question my motives for making them talk this way.

Grossberg is correct to point out that the regime of communication is not a description at all, but rather the logic of a particular framework which Reddy (1979) calls the "conduit metaphor." When Reddy refers to a logic, he is not referring to a formal, developed logical system, but rather an informal, cultural logic informed by our use of the English language. It is the logic demonstrated by our use of everyday English expressions which people employ to describe the communication process. Reddy identifies four categories which constitute the major framework of the conduit metaphor:

- Language functions like a conduit, transferring thoughts bodily from one person to another.

- In writing and speaking, people insert their thoughts or feelings into the words.

- Words accomplish the transfer by containing the thoughts or feelings and conveying them to others.

- In listening or reading, people extract the thoughts and feelings once again from the words.

It is clear from our discussions that my students cling strongly to these general principles. Indeed it is very difficult to talk about communication any other way since, if one agrees with Grossberg and Reddy, it is built into their very language. As Reddy (1979) points out, "the logic of the framework runs like threads in many directions through the syntactic and semantic fabric of our speech habits. Merely becoming cognizant of this in no way alters the situation" (p. 297).

The subject of this book is Grossberg's (1997) "regime of communication": the ways in which people, lay people and academics alike, talk about and create the reality that is the transmission view of communication. The book will follow a line of inquiry inspired by the Austrian philosopher Ludwig Wittgenstein (1980), who wrote that:

When I say "I remembered, I believed . . . ," don't ask yourself "What fact, what process is he remembering?". . . ask rather "What is the purpose of this language, how is it being used?" (p. 131)

This book will follow a similar sentiment. A student who says "I communicated a message to my friend" will be typically concerned with the nature of the message being sent and the accuracy with which that message was received. They will not be concerned with the utterance itself. However, following Wittgenstein, this book will focus on the utterances like "I communicated a message to my friend." It will ask questions like: Why does the student speak this way? What is the purpose of producing utterances of this kind? How is it being used? Grossberg (1997) writes of being "perturbed by the lack of reflection on how and why the concept [of communication] has been deployed, on the genealogy of the concept itself" (p. 27). This book will offer such a reflection on how and why we *deploy* communication in the context of both everyday and academic speech.

A reflection of this kind requires a radically different way of approaching communication as a subject matter. In my classes, students are concerned with the following question:

> What is the nature of the reality to which our talk and theories about communication refers?

Being able to articulate this reality will enable them to become better communicators. However, the question being posed in this book is very different:

> Why do we *talk* about communication using the vocabulary of transmission and conduits?

In treating the transmission theory of communication as a discourse rather than as a phenomenon, our interest lies not in investigating whether such communication is valid, testable, reliable, misleading, has effects, or can change behaviors. Such questions and their investigation serve to *generate and sustain* the discourse. In a sense, it is already known that communication exists because it exists in and through the discourse that sustains it. The question becomes the discourse itself.

As a reader, I realize you will be approaching this book with certain expectations. Maybe you are expecting a review of pertinent theories in the field of communication. Maybe you are expecting a history of the communication concept, or the role of communication in a contemporary globalized society. This book is none of those things. It refuses to see communication as a thing or a process at all. The objective of this book is to produce a discourse about the discourse of communication. It is precisely this objective, and the manner by which such a discourse of discourses can be produced, that formed the major problematic in the work of the late French philosopher Michel Foucault. For example, in *The Order of Things*,

Foucault (1973) attempted to specify a discourse by which one can understand the discourses of the human sciences. He was not concerned with what those discourses talk *about*, but rather the discourses themselves, and how they function to produce the objects of knowledge that are then studied by social scientists. The same can be said concerning the discourses of "sexuality" in *The History of Sexuality* (Foucault, 1980). Foucault sought to avoid becoming involved in arguments about what the human sciences say is true, or even whether their statements make sense. Rather he proposes to "treat all that is said in the human sciences as a 'discourse object'" (Dreyfus & Rabinow, 1983, p. xxiv).

In this book, I shall follow Foucault's lead and regard the transmission view of communication as a *discourse object*. To understand the discourse of communication, it is necessary to put aside notions of what communication is (i.e., how the word/concept relates to the world) and focus instead on what is said, and why it is said. I will refer to this transmission discourse using Grossberg's term-"the regime of communication."

The regime of communication enables my students to provide answers to the questions I pose in my class. It enables the lay person to understand what they are doing when they make a telephone call to a friend, or send a postcard from their vacation. It enables people in the communication professions to understand what they are doing when they write and send out a press release, compose an article for a newspaper, or do the graphic design work on a brochure. They know they are translating ideas in their mind into a message that will cause a response in those to whom the message is sent.

But where did this particular regime of communication come from? If not the world, from where does it draw its resources? Why do we speak about communication this way and not some other way? What is the relationship between this way of speaking about communication and our experience of ourselves, of others, and of the world? Is it possible to speak about communication in some other way and still make sense? These are the questions addressed in this book.

The Structure of the Book

As you read this book, you will find that much of it is taken with a discussion of cognitive psychology. The reason for this is that the regime of communication articulated by my students draws heavily on a psychological view of themselves and the world. My students tell me communication begins in the mind of a sender and ends in the mind of a receiver. This talk of minds draws heavily on a psychological discourse in which mental processes determine who we are and what we do. My students use the discourse of psychology as a resource in building their own accounts of communication. My students are not unique in this. Communication scholars in the 1940s and 1950s also used psychological talk as a basis for articulating the appropriate subject matter of the new academic discipline of communication studies.

This book looks at other discursive resources upon which our articulation and understanding of communication draws. Paramount among these is the empiricist account of the human understanding provided by John Locke (1690/1975), which is the subject of Chapter Two. Locke's consideration of language and communication was tangential to his account of ideas, knowledge, and the human understanding. However, he made one claim that was to become the mainstay of communication discourse; that words "cast a mist before our eyes" (Locke, 1690/1975, p. 488; Book III, Chapter IX, xxi). For Locke, all communication is inherently imperfect. It is fundamentally impossible to communicate accurately the ideas in the mind of one person to stimulate exactly the same ideas in the mind of another person.

Chapter Three examines the discourse of the unconscious as articulated by such figures as Eduard von Hartmann, Frederick Myers, William James, and Sigmund Freud and how the unconscious provided the means to articulate a scientific account of human inner experience. I also examine how the invocation of the unconscious forms the basis of the information processing model within modern cognitive psychology, which provides the dominant metaphor my students employ in their articulation of communication.

Chapter Four examines the profound impact of the mathematical theory of communication developed by Claude E. Shannon (1949). I say profound, not because of the insights that Shannon offered in this theory, but in the manner that Shannon's theory legitimated a whole realm of discourse that could describe communication as a subject in terms that were scientifically legitimate. Of more importance than Shannon is the introduction to Shannon's theory written by Warren Weaver (1949), who showed us not what communication was, but how we could talk about communication in a scientifically legitimate way. As Peters (1986) argues:

> While communication was trying to carve out an institutional place for itself in universities during the 1950s and 1960s, something else was happening in intellectual life that served to elevate the fortunes of "communication"-information theory. The field's use of information theory illustrates the victory of

institution over intellect in the formation of the field, because the theory was used almost exclusively for purposes of legitimation. The interesting ideas that information theory stimulated, in contrast, have generally had little profound or coherent intellectual impact on the field. (p. 83)

This chapter also examines the convergence of information processing and information theory in Norbert Wiener's (1954) theory of cybernetics, which provided the linguistic resources necessary to view communication as a means of control.

Chapter Five considers the impact communication discourse has made on psychological discourse. My students use the discourse of psychology as a means of articulating their understanding of communication. However, as the two discourses merge, the opposite also happens; the discourse of communication comes to inform our understanding of ourselves as information processors. In this chapter I use the work of experimental psychologists Elizabeth Loftus and Norman F. Dixon as examples to show how a Lockean-derived model of communication comes to influence the discourse of psychology as it attempts to describe the information processing routines of the mind.

Chapter Six asks the question: how can we escape the regime of communication and speak about communication in some other way? Since our discourse structures our realities, this is no easy task. We take as our guides Ludwig Wittgenstein (1958) and the character of O'Brien from George Orwell's (1949/1984) novel *1984*. Many of the beliefs my students offer concerning communication and its relationship to their ideas and memories are reflected in the beliefs of Winston Smith, Orwell's protagonist in *1984*. O'Brien employs techniques of extreme torture to train Winston to speak and think in new ways. I suggest something similar is needed to produce a similar understanding in my students.

Chapter Seven asks us to imagine a communication theory that makes no reference to the human mind. The regime of communication has conditioned us into seeing communication as a product of our minds, and to believing that an understanding of communication can be achieved only through an understanding of the mind that makes it possible. By this point in the book, I hope to have demonstrated that our belief in the mind as the basis of communication is not built on facts, but on the discursive resources available to us as we attempt to articulate our understanding of communication. The discursive resources that dominate our contemporary ways of speaking about communication are those provided by psychology, both ancient and modern. In this chapter, I offer a different set of discursive resources, the semiotic theory of Umberto Eco and the *Logical Investigations* of Edmund Husserl (1900/1970), in which it is possible to conceive and speak about communication in ways that do not depend on a discourse of mind.

Chapter Eight offers another set of discursive resources for the articulation of communication: hermeneutics. The discourse of European theorists Wilhelm Dilthey and Hans-Georg Gadamer is presented as a means of eclipsing the dominant psychological discourse of the regime of communication by using *conversation*, rather than transmission, as the central metaphor.

The book concludes with Chapter Nine where we return to the idea that our knowledge of communication is contained within the language we use to speak about it. Concepts such as "thought," "idea," "encoding," "transmission," and "decoding," all of which come so easily in the accounts of my students, can only derive their significance and their appearance of reality from the context of the discourse in which they appear. By the end of this book, it is hoped that you will have gained a clearer understanding of the resources you instinctively rely on when you articulate your own understanding of the term "communication." It is also hoped that you will be able to articulate alternative ways of articulating and understanding communication that will take you beyond the limits of Grossberg's (1997) "regime of communication."

Two
John Locke and the Transmission Model of Communication:
A Mist Before Our Eyes

> *To make Words serviceable to the end of Communication, it is necessary . . . that they excite, in the Hearer, exactly the same Idea, they stand for in the Mind of the speaker. (John Locke)*

The discussions I have with my students make it clear that they consider the regime of communication to be a very natural and common sense view. They lack the historical sense that the use of communication in a transmission vocabulary is a relatively recent development. Just a quick glance at the entry for "communication" in the *Oxford English Dictionary* (*OED*) (1933) makes it very clear that the transmission view is not the only way one can use "communication" in discourse.

James Carey (1992) points out that there are two major conceptions of communication that have been alive in American culture since the term entered common discourse in the nineteenth century. The first is the transmission view of communication as expressed by my students. The second is what Carey calls a ritual view of communication. The ritual view is by far the older of the two.

In the ritual view, "communication" is firmly linked to terms such as "sharing," "participation," and "association" rather than "transmission." It draws a direct line from its roots of "commonness," "communion," and "community" in ways that the *OED* now lists as archaic. As Carey (1992) describes: "A ritual view of communication is directed not toward the extension of messages in space but toward the maintenance of society in time; not the act of imparting information but the representation of shared beliefs" (p. 18). The archetypal case of "communication" is not the sender transmitting a message to the receiver, but the sacred ceremony that draws people together in fellowship and commonality, such as Holy Communion. In the ritual view, importance is placed upon the role of community prayer, singing, and the ceremony, and not upon the individual priest who gives the sermon to a congregation.

The ritual view of communication dominates the definitions of "communication" found in the *OED*. One finds "communication" related to the term "communion," which refers to "mutual participation and fellowship" and "the sharing or holding in common with others." Similarly, the term "commune" is "to make common" or "to share." Current senses of "commune" include to "talk together" or "to converse." Again, the dominant sense here is the idea of sharing through the activity of talking. "Communication" as it is used in conjunction with "communion" is to "unite in celebration or observance of the Lord's Supper." Similarly, the adjective "communicative" refers to a person being "open to familiar intercourse, sociable, not stiff or reserved; to be free in conversation, open, and talkative." It describes a person capable of being social and of sharing.

"Communication" is also related to the term "common": "belonging equally to more than one; possessed or shared alike by both or all; free to be used by everyone." For example, the *OED* (1933) offers the following definition of "common" which is now considered to be archaic:

> To communicate, to impart, to share with; to communicate verbally, tell, declare, publish, report; to take part in common with others; to participate, share with; to associate with. (Volume II, p. 700)

But this is not how we use "communication" today. Something happened to shift this ritual view of "communication" and its links with "commune," "communion," and "community" into relative obsolescence. According to Raymond Williams (1983), a shift occurred in the late fifteenth century where "communication" not only referred to the *action* of making common, but also the *object* thus made common; i.e., *a* communication.

This second sense of "communication" has remained dominant to this day. From the late seventeenth century, there was an important extension of the term to cover the *means* of communication. "Communications" was often the general abstract term for the physical facilities of roads, canals, and railways. In the twentieth and twenty-first centuries, "communications" came to refer to other means of passing information and maintaining social contact, such as the press and broadcast media. In modern usage, the communications industry is usually distinguished from the transport industry with "communications" being used for the transmission of information and ideas in print and broadcasting, and "transport" being used for the physical movement of people and goods. It is clear from the use of "communication" through the past centuries that the transmission sense of the term has come to dominate the communion sense. Reflecting upon why the term "communication" has become such a problematic term in modern academic discourse, Williams (1983) remarks that it is:

> Often useful to recall the unresolved range of the original noun of action, represented at its extremes by *transmit*, a one-way process, and *share* (cf. **communion** and especially **communicant**), a common or mutual process. The intermediate senses-make common to many, and impart-can be read in either direction, and the choice of direction is often crucial. (pp. 72-73)

My students, guided by the regime of communication, invariably tend toward the transmission extreme of Williams's continuum. The question I want to address in this chapter is: Why is this so? At least part of the answer can be found in the works of the English empiricist philosopher John Locke and his *An Essay Concerning Human Understanding* (Locke, 1690/1975).

An Essay Concerning Human Understanding

Whenever we set out to think or discourse seriously about communication, we almost always find ourselves reenacting a philosophical . . . drama first written by John Locke. (John Durham Peters)

The *OED* (1933) defines the modern transmission sense of the term "communication" as follows:

The imparting, conveying, or exchange of ideas, knowledge, information, etc. (whether by speech, writing, or signs). (Volume II, p. 700)

The *OED* provides examples of the usage of this sense and gives references to those texts where this sense was first used. In the case of the transmission sense of "communication," the first and earliest citation that is given is John Locke's (1690/1975) *An Essay Concerning Human Understanding*. The example from Locke cited by the *OED* (1933) is the sentence fragment:

To make Words serviceable to the end of Communication. (Volume II, p. 700)

The complete paragraph from which this sentence fragment is taken describes a view of communication that could have been uttered by any modern student:

To make Words serviceable to the end of Communication, it is necessary . . . that they excite, in the Hearer, exactly the same Idea, they stand for in the Mind of the speaker. Without this, Men fill one another's Heads with noise and sounds; but convey not thereby their Thoughts, and lay not before one another their Ideas, which is the end of Discourse and Language (Locke, 1690/1975, p. 478; Book III, Chapter IX, xi).

As Locke uses the term, "communication" becomes a conduit for the exciting of ideas in the mind of a hearer that correspond to the ideas in the mind of a speaker. The sense of *conveying* an idea replaces the older sense of *sharing* an idea. The respective roles of the initiator of movement (a speaker) and the destination (a hearer) become integral parts of the definition. This nuance is a subtle but an extremely important shift.

Locke's use of the term "excite," as in words "exciting" in the hearer the same idea as that in the mind of a speaker, invokes a mechanical rather than a community metaphor. Locke's description invokes the image of an electrical current passing between two points and causing a light to be activated at the destination. Indeed, the image of the light bulb representing someone having an idea follows perfectly from this description.

Locke's discussion of communication was completely ancillary to his main interest in writing the *Essay*, which was an investigation of the role of the Human Understanding in the production of knowledge. Locke

(1690/1975) writes that: "When I first began this Discourse of the Understanding, and a good while after, I had not the least Thought, that any Consideration of Words was at all necessary to it" (p. 488; III, IX, 21). Yet it was Locke's use of the term "communication" in his *Essay* that was to form the decisive shift to the modern sense of the term that now dominates the discourse of my students. To understand Locke's use of "communication," it is necessary to place it back in the context of his main thesis concerning the nature of the Human Understanding. As we shall see, many of Locke's concerns mirror those I regularly discuss with my students.

Locke's Account of Knowledge

Locke's *An Essay Concerning Human Understanding* is often identified as the seminal account of an empiricist theory of knowledge. Nidditch (1975) remarks that "the *Essay* gained for itself a unique standing as the most thorough and plausible formulation of empiricism-a viewpoint that it caused to become an enduring powerful force" (p. vii). The basis of Locke's view of knowledge is clearly explained. Locke (1690/1975) writes:

> Let us then suppose the Mind to be, as we say, white paper, void of all Characters, without any *Ideas*; How comes it to be furnished? Whence comes it by that vast store, which the busy and boundless Fancy of Man has painted on it, with an almost endless variety? Whence has it all the materials of Reason and Knowledge. (p. 104; Book II, Chapter I, ii)

Locke offers the following thesis:

> To this I answer, in one word, from *Experience*: In that, all our Knowledge is founded; and from that it ultimately derives itself. Our Observations employ'd either about *external, sensible Objects; or about the internal Operations of our Minds, perceived and reflected upon by our selves, is that, which supplies our Understanding with all the materials of thinking.* These two are the Fountains of Knowledge, from whence all the Ideas we have, or can naturally have, do spring. (p. 104; Book II, Chapter I, ii)

Locke's problem of genuine knowledge has much in common with the rationalist thesis of Rene Descartes (1641/1984). Both Descartes and Locke have as their starting point a blank mind devoid of ideas, presuppositions, and knowledge. Descartes conceived of such a state through a method of radical doubt; suppose everything I know is false, or an illusion, or the product of a deceiver? Once the mind has been cleared of the clutter of thought derived from uncertain sources, including those of the senses, what knowledge is left that is totally and utterly reliable? What knowledge can be found that simply cannot be doubted?

Locke also begins with the premise of a clear and empty mind-the famous *tabula rasa*. However, in Locke's case, the *tabula rasa* is not a state to be achieved by the philosopher, as in Descartes's method. Rather, it is a state that is assumed to exist at the beginning of every human's life: "Let us then suppose the Mind to be," Locke suggests, "as we say, white paper, void of all Characters, without any *Ideas*." The question then arises: "How comes it to be furnished?"

For Locke, the *tabula rasa* is written on by experience collected by the senses. Perception begins with an object in the world, say a tree. Light signals bounce off the tree and are collected by the eyes. The eyes send a signal to the mind and, using this material, the mind is able to produce a representation of the tree. The direct experience of the tree by the mind is a "simple idea"; an immediate sense datum that, in itself, cannot be defined. It is the experience produced before reflection and definition takes place: the silky feel of a cat's fur, the sweet taste of an apple, the glowing colors of a sunset. All simple ideas are fundamentally asocial and alinguistic. They are not the product of convention, culture, or vocabulary. They are pure sense data that reflect the nature of the objects that caused the experience. Locke will trace all genuine, as opposed to spurious, knowledge to a foundation of simple ideas that have passed into the mind through the inlets of the senses.

The transmission view of communication is entirely consistent with this picture. The receiver in the transmission view is often portrayed as a *tabula rasa*, a slate on which will be written the ideas of a sender. But, as Locke notes, it is not only the reception of physical signals (sound, for example) that defines communication. "Men fill one another's Heads with noise and sounds," Locke (1690/1975) writes, "but convey not thereby their Thoughts . . . which is the end of Discourse and Language" (p. 478; Book III, Chapter IX, xi). Locke clearly differentiates between the physical form of words (sounds, marks on a page) and the thoughts that they are intended to convey. This differentiation is totally consistent with the modern conduit metaphor whose logic suggests that the act of communication involves putting ideas *into* words. The words then convey the idea to the receiver who takes it *out* of the words. As Reddy (1979) has argued, this way of talking about communication leads to the "bizarre assertion that words must have 'insides' and 'outsides.' After all, if thoughts can be 'inserted,' there must be a space 'inside' where meaning can reside" (p. 288). This distinction between the perceptual experience of a word as a sound (a simple idea) and the experience of the word as the conveyor of a meaning is representative of Locke's overall thesis on the nature of knowledge.

Locke suggests that the senses provide the mind with a pure experience of a tree. If the simple idea of the tree is considered as a mental picture produced in the mind by the senses, what is it that looks at this picture and decides what it is? Locke (1690/1975) proposes that our idea of the tree is the result of an interaction between the representation of the tree caused by the object and the "the internal Operations of our Minds, perceived and reflected upon by our selves" (p. 104; Book II, Chapter I, ii). The mental faculty which carries out this internal perception and reflection is the Human Understanding, which is the basis of Locke's famous *Essay*. The Understanding is a faculty of the mind which the subject uses to apprehend its objects.

Locke understood that perception is an act of the mind and is not simply a passive receptor or mirror of the external world. The Human Understanding provides an interface between the mind and the world. It works on incoming sense data to create acts and objects of perception. In its time, this view was incredibly empowering for individuals. With his notion of the simple idea being a pure, asocial, and alinguistic experience, Locke was suggesting that individuals can see things "as they are" and not as presented by the dominant institutions of the church, crown, or custom. Locke's view minimized the social or intersubjective aspects of human knowing. It emphasized the power of the individual to create understandings and make sense of the world based on unique data provided to her by her own senses.

We can see here the groundwork of the view my students express that communication is concerned with individuals rather than groups or communities. For my students, it is the individual who has an idea; it is the individual who decides how to encode that idea into symbols; and it is the individual who decides how the message will be transmitted. On the receiver side of the equation, it is an individual mind that receives the message, and an individual mind that interprets and understands the meanings contained within that message. The idea that is both sent and received is a property of the individual, not of the society or culture. When I ask how understanding is possible between two individual minds, the students are quick to explain that each mind has stored within it a set of common symbols and vocabulary upon which it can draw. But, again, this knowledge of language is contained *within* the individual mind, and decisions regarding access and use of that knowledge is made by the individual.

The transmission view articulated by my students recognizes that the idea received by the receiver is never an exact copy of the one contained in the mind of the sender. The receiver hears the sender's words as *simple ideas* (in Locke's sense) of noise and sound. The idea itself must be *extracted* by a mental faculty equivalent to Locke's Human Understanding. My students usually call this a process of interpretation. They recognize, as did Locke, that meaning is created in the receiver through the interaction of perceptual data and some internal operation of internal reflection. Meanings are never sent directly from sender to receiver.

The Communication of Genuine Knowledge

The interaction of simple ideas and the Human Understanding form the basis of Locke's consideration of "genuine knowledge." Simple ideas provide the subject with a rudimentary knowledge of the subject's immediate environment: what the subject can see, hear, touch, taste, and smell. Genuine knowledge comes through creation of complex ideas.

Complex ideas are created through the addition, subtraction, combination, and arrangement of simple ideas. The mind is passive in the reception of simple ideas, but active in making complex ideas from simple ones. Locke understood that complex ideas are both necessary and dangerous. They are the road to meaningful knowledge. However, they are also the source of intellectual monstrosities. People are free to dream up unicorns, square circles, centaurs, spirits, and much more. Within this observation can be found the main purpose of Locke's *Essay*. Locke does not set out to describe a mechanism by which the mind is able to perceive and understand. Rather, he wants to identify those criteria by which the mind can differentiate between complex ideas which are genuine, and those complex ideas which are fantasy and imagination. Locke (1690/1975) articulates the project this way: "this, therefore, being my Purpose to enquire into the Original Certainty, and Extent of humane Knowledge" (p. 43; Book I, Chapter I, ii).

We find a similar problem embedded in the logic of modern transmission views of communication. If a receiver's understanding of a message is always a creation of the receiver, how does a sender know or guarantee that this interpretation is a genuine reflection of the sender's idea and that this idea is not just fantasy? For Locke, there are *limits to what the mind can know with certainty.* Locke's goal is the identification of those limits:

> We should not then perhaps be so forward, out of an Affectation of an universal Knowledge, to raise Questions, and perplex our selves and others with Disputes about Things, to which our Understandings are not suited; and of which we cannot frame in our Minds any clear or distinct Perceptions, or whereof (as it perhaps too often happen'd) we have not any Notions at all. If we can find out, how far the Understanding can extend its view; how far it has faculties to attain Certainty; and in what Cases it can only judge and guess, we may learn to content our selves with what is attainable by us in this State. (Locke, 1690/1975, p. 45; Book I, Chapter I, iv)

Locke asks: What are the limits of those ideas we can know with certainty? What are the limits of the faculty by which understanding of those ideas is achieved? Can we be content with that knowledge attained in this state, and resist the urge to seek knowledge that the human faculties are not equipped to deal with? Locke (1690/1975) continues:

> Thus Men, extending their Enquiries beyond their Capacities, and letting their Thoughts wander into those depths where they can find no sure Footing: 'tis no Wonder, that they raise Questions, and multiply Disputes, which never coming to any clear Resolution, are proper only to continue and increase their Doubts, and to confirm them at last in perfect Skepticism. Whereas were the Capacities of our Understandings well considered, the Extent of our Knowledge once discovered, and the Horizon found, which sets the Bounds between the enlightened and dark part of Things; between what is, and what is not comprehensible by us, Men would perhaps with less scruple acquiesce in the avow'd Ignorance of the one, and imploy their Thoughts and Discourse, with more Advantage and Satisfaction in the other. (p. 47; Book I, Chapter I, vii)

Like Descartes, Locke seeks a reliable foundation for knowledge; a foundation which stays within the bounds of what the faculty of human understanding is capable of knowing with certainty. Both seek the foundations of what Locke terms "clear and distinct perceptions" and both seek to avoid the epistemological dead-end of a perfect skepticism, where everything is doubted and certain knowledge is unattainable. As Descartes attempted to formulate a method by which certain knowledge could be identified and generated in the sciences and other realms, so Locke is looking to articulate those criteria which will enable us to identify those claims to knowledge which fall within the boundaries of the human understanding, and those which fall outside.

Locke's use of the term "communication" is informed directly by these concerns. Thus, he differentiated between *two kinds of communication*: a slippery communication for everyday use and a rigorous philosophical communication for expressing truth. The everyday transmission of ideas from one mind to another is referred to by Locke (1690/1975) as "civil," which he defines as:

> Such communication of Thoughts and *Ideas* by Words, as may serve for the upholding common Conversation and Commerce, about the ordinary Affairs and Conveniences of civil life, in the Societies of Men, one amongst another. (p. 476; Book III, Chapter IX, iii)

Civil communication is the means by which people relate to each other in their social and cultural lives. It is much closer to the older ritual views of communication than it is to the transmission view. It stresses the role of communication in the "ordinary Affairs and Conveniences of civil life" and for the upholding of common conversation. This role is not the kind of communication Locke is interested in, and we see here his need to invoke a *new* kind of communication.

Locke's new conception of communication is not concerned with civil life or everyday conversation. He needs to address the means by which genuine knowledge can be passed from one person to another, or one generation to another, in a manner that is accurate and preserves the truth of the ideas being conveyed. Locke refers to this form of communication as "philosophical." It refers to such a use of words:

> As may serve to convey the precise Notions of Things, and to express, in general Propositions, certain and undoubted Truths, which the Mind may rest upon, and be satisfied with, in its search after true knowledge. (Locke, 1690/1975, p. 476; Book III, Chapter IX, iii)

It is in the philosophical use of words that we find the modern preoccupation with communication as the matching of ideas in a sender and receiver. If communication is to be considered successful, the transfer of ideas needs to be accurate. The idea I hold in my mind must match to some significant degree the idea you hold in your mind. If it doesn't match, then we have a case of miscommunication. This concern is the same one faced by Locke when he spoke of the role of philosophical communication as being "to convey the precise Notions of Things" such that "the Mind may rest upon, and be satisfied with, in its search after true knowledge." True knowledge must be the same true knowledge no matter who receives it. Ideally, there should be no difference in the mind of a sender or a receiver of a true and genuine idea.

A Mist Before Our Eyes

[Words] interpose themselves so much between our Understandings, and the Truth, which it would contemplate and apprehend, that like the Medium through which visible Objects pass, their Obscurity and Disorder does not seldom cast a mist before our Eyes, and impose upon our Understandings. (John Locke)

The most significant conclusion to be drawn from Locke's account of communication is that words and signs are imperfect vehicles for the transmission of ideas. Communication is not a tool that can be used and exploited. For Locke, communication is a fundamental problem the consequences of which need to be recognized and minimized. Locke's view that communication is a fundamental problem drives much of contemporary discourse about communication. My students often point out that if perfect communication could be achieved, i.e., if there could be an absolute correspondence obtained between the ideas of a sender and the ideas of a receiver, then advertising executives would have produced the perfect commercial years ago and retired to the South of France.

My students recognize Locke's claim that communication can never be perfect. Couples continue to misunderstand each other. People vote for the other candidate despite the best produced campaign commercials. Students continue to get C and D grades despite having wonderful professors and clearly written textbooks. If communication were a perfect process, understanding would be total, and all students would get A grades all the time. The world would live in constant state of peace and contentment. But these things do not happen, and one reason that is given for this is that communication is imperfect. For Locke (1690/1975), words:

Interpose themselves so much between our Understandings, and the Truth, which it would contemplate and apprehend, that like the *Medium* through which visible Objects pass, their Obscurity and Disorder does not seldom cast a mist before our Eyes, and impose upon our Understandings. (p. 488; Book III, Chapter IX, xxi)

Locke clearly differentiates here between the "truth" and our "understanding" of the truth. For Locke, words do not make the truth more apparent to our understanding. Quite the opposite. Words impose "Obscurity and Disorder" which does not "seldom cast a mist before our eyes." Words do not reveal truth to our understanding, they act as a fundamental impediment. Such a situation clearly represents a significant problem for a philosopher like Locke who is attempting to discover fundamental truths concerning the Human Understanding and then, horrors, is forced to transmit these truths to others by a communication process that is intrinsically imperfect and unreliable.

Locke's contemporary, George Berkeley, also introduces language as a major concern in his consideration of the first principles of human knowledge. Berkeley (1710/1975), like Locke, considers the use of words in communication to be a *fundamental obstacle* to the articulation of clear and distinct ideas: "it must be owned that most parts of knowledge have been strangely perplexed and darkened by the abuse of words, and general ways of speech wherein they are delivered" (p. 85). How can Berkeley or Locke be expected to communicate the first principles of knowledge using language systems that only serve to obscure, perplex, and make ambiguous? Berkeley is the first to admit that this is no easy task. It would require a philosophical method which presupposes "an entire deliverance from the deception of words, which I dare hardly promise myself; so difficult a thing it is to dissolve an union so early begun, and confirmed by so long a habit as that betwixt words and ideas" (p. 86).

Berkeley's (1710/1975) only solution is to offer the reader a warning in his introduction as to the nature and abuse of language and to encourage the reader to adopt a radical skepticism of words:

Unless we take care to clear the first principles of knowledge, from the embarrass and delusion of words, we may make infinite reasonings upon them to no purpose; we may draw consequences from consequences, and be never the wiser. The farther we go, we shall only lose ourselves the more irrecoverably. (p. 86)

25

Communication Breakdown

Communication breakdown
It's always the same
Having a nervous breakdown
Drive me insane.
(Jimmy Page, John Paul Jones & John Bonham)

The whole problem of communication hinges on the fact that people cannot communicate their ideas directly and in a pure form. As Locke (1690/1975) points out, a man's thoughts "all within his own Breast, invisible, and hidden from others, nor can themselves be made appear" (p. 404, Book III, Chapter II, I). Thus Locke identifies a double use for words: (a) "for the recording of our own Thoughts," and (b) "for the Communicating of our Thoughts to others" (p. 476; Book III, Chapter IX, I).

In the first use, words can be used to record our thoughts with the help of memory. Any word will do. Since sounds are voluntary, a person may use whatever words she pleases to signify her ideas to herself, as long as she uses the same words consistently. Here Locke recognizes the arbitrary nature of the relationship between signs and ideas, which will become a central component of modern semiotic theory:

> We may conceive how Words . . . come to be made use of by Man, as *the Signs of their Ideas*; not by any natural connexion, that there is between particular articulate Sounds and certain *Ideas*, for then there would be but one Language amongst all Men; but by a voluntary Imposition, whereby such a Word is made arbitrarily the Mark of such an *Idea*. (Locke, 1690/1975, p. 405; Book III, Chapter II, I)

The ability of the individual to assign words to express ideas is thus a source of empowerment. However, it is also the cause of potential misunderstandings between a sender and a receiver. As Locke (1690/1975) recognizes: "Every Man has so inviolable a Liberty, to makes Words stand for what *Ideas* he pleases, that no one hath the Power to make others have the same *Ideas* in their Minds, that he has, when they use the same Words, that he does" (p. 408; Book III, Chapter II, viii). Just because a sender can employ a certain word to stand for a particular idea, she has no way of knowing if the receiver allocates that same word to the same idea or a different idea.

26

In 1969, the rock band Led Zeppelin expressed the same idea in their song "Communication Breakdown" (Page, Jones & Bonham, 1969):

Communication breakdown
It's always the same
Having a nervous breakdown
Drive me insane

For both Locke and Led Zeppelin (did you ever expect to see that pairing of names in a scholarly book on communication?), communication breakdown is the natural state of affairs whenever people attempt to convey their ideas or feelings. As Led Zeppelin sings, "it's always the same." Communication breakdown is inevitable for both John Locke and Jimmy Page.

There are at least two ways in which to read "Communication Breakdown," both of which are appropriate to the Lockean discussion of communication. The first is the idea of breakdown as "failure," of communication going wrong, of becoming dysfunctional. A second reading of communication breakdown is the notion that communication is a problem precisely because, as a process, it is "broken down" into various stages. Communication is not a direct process of transmission from speaker to hearer. Ideas have to be produced, words have to be assigned, messages have to be transmitted, and meaning has to be extracted. Because of all these intermediate stages, the idea that the receiver forms in her mind as a result of being exposed to the sender's message is not, nor could it ever be with any certainty, the same as the idea originally conceived in the mind of the sender. This uncertainty is enough to drive one to a "nervous breakdown"; it is enough to "drive me insane" (Page, Jones & Bonham, 1969).

Consider the transmission view of communication. The individual has an idea that she wants to express to another. To do this she must encode that idea in language, which can then be transmitted as a message. The sender has the liberty *to choose* the words, sentences, and phrases in which that idea will be encoded. You will very likely be familiar with the situation in which you find it difficult to find the "right words" to express your ideas. When writing an essay, a letter to a friend, or an email message, you may find yourself tearing up rough drafts or deleting files in frustration because they will not say what you want them to say. I suffered the same frustration in the writing of this book, and I had to write and rewrite several drafts before I was even remotely happy with it.

This problem arises because there is no single or obvious way of expressing the ideas you wish to communicate. For any expression that may come to mind, there are always ways to revise, expand, and paraphrase. For any idea you wish to communicate, there is always a choice of how the message can be encoded. There is never a one-to-one correspondence between the thought and its expression. For any idea there is a choice of what you're going to say and how it is going to be said.

For example, consider what you would say if you were asked to describe something fun you did over the weekend to the following people: (a) your father, (b) a good male friend, (c) a good female friend, and (d) your eight-year-old nephew. You might also consider how you would describe this event: (a) the day after it happened, (b) a week after it happened, and (c) a month after it happened. This little thought experiment should lead you to conclude that your descriptions of what is objectively one and the same event will be quite, if not very, different. Which of these accounts might be considered the "correct" one, or at least the most "accurate?" In a sense, they are all correct. They are all encoding the same event, or memory of that event, but the encodings themselves can be quite different. Only you have access to the idea in question and the events as they happened. The people you tell about it only have recourse to the accounts you give them, and these accounts can vary according to the context of its telling, who it is being told to, and how long after the event the account is given.

As I write this text, I look down at my feet and see my daughter's pet cat, Lucifer. I say to myself, "my goodness, you certainly are a beautiful cat." I return to my computer and I type:

My cat is beautiful.

You now have my book in your hands and you are reading the words I wrote many months, maybe many years, ago. Does the sentence "My cat is beautiful" clearly express to you the thought or perception I had in mind when I wrote these words? You can receive "some" idea but I would argue that it is not "the" idea. Indeed, as I myself read these words again some six months after originally writing them, I cannot recall or invoke that original idea.

There is also a wealth of information about my daughter's cat that is simply excluded from this phrase. What kind of cat is Lucifer? What makes him so beautiful? His coat? His face? Why is he called Lucifer? More to the point, why am I talking about my daughter's cat anyway? As an example? Why not say "I see a tree" or "I see a computer monitor" or "I see my hands typing on my keyboard"? If the point is simply to give an example, then the reference to some particular cat is irrelevant since this is not the idea I want to express. What actually is the idea behind "my cat is beautiful"? Working backwards from words to ideas is a difficult business, if only because the ideas thus identified must be encoded in words, which themselves express ideas, and so on. The words I choose to express ideas are not exact fits and rarely, if ever, perfect fits. This choice is the first transformation the idea has to make and the first fundamental problem of communication.

As Locke has pointed out, "to make Words serviceable to the end of Communication, it is necessary that they excite, in the Hearer, exactly the same Idea, they stand for in the Mind of the speaker. Without this," Locke continues, "Men fill one another's Heads with noise and sounds." The stories I tell of my fun weekend and my daughter's cat are only so much sound I make with my lips or marks I make on paper with my computer. I know how they stand in relation to my ideas and to my experience. But my listeners cannot know or experience this. My internal mental states are inaccessible to them. So it is not enough that I talk and make sounds. I must be able to *use these sounds* as signs of my ideas so that my thoughts might be conveyed to another. Locke (1690/1975) expresses this as follows:

> Besides articulate Sounds therefore, it was farther necessary, that he should be *able to use the sounds, as Signs of internal Conceptions*; and to make them stand as marks for the *Ideas* within his own Mind, whereby they might be made known to others, and the Thoughts of Men's Minds be conveyed from one to another. (p. 402; Book III, Chapter I, ii)

However, because of the arbitrary relationship between words and ideas, the gulf between the thought, the sign, and the ideas of the receiver is monumental and, ultimately, insurmountable. Communication breakdown-it's always the same. Locke (1690/1975) elaborates this theme in his discussion of simple ideas and why one can not use language to communicate to the hearer the simple ideas experienced by a sender:

> *Simple Ideas*, as has been shewn, *are only* to be *got by* those *impressions* Objects themselves make on our Minds, by the proper Inlets appointed to each sort. If they are not received this way, all the *Words* in the World, *made use of to explain, or define any of their Names, will never be able to produce in us the* Idea *it stands for*. For Words, being Sounds, can produce in us no other Simple *Ideas*, than of those very Sounds (p. 424; Book III, Chapter IV, xi).

To understand Locke's claim, try to explain to someone else your perception of redness or the taste of a pineapple. You can provide more words as examples. You might say "red is the color of an apple" or "the taste of a pineapple is sweet, like an orange." You can say what the simple idea *is like*, but you cannot convey what the simple idea *is*.

A similar problem arises when one tries to communicate a complex idea such as "freedom," "evil," or "God." Locke (1690/1975) argues that:

> When a word stands for a very complex *Idea*, that is compounded and decompounded, it is not easy for Men to form and retain that *Idea* so exactly, as to make the Name in common use, stand for the same precise *Idea*, without any of the least variation. Hence it comes to pass, that Men's Names, of very compound *Ideas*, such as for the most part are moral Words, have seldom, in two different Men, the same precise signification; since one Man's complex *Idea* seldom agrees with anothers, and often differs from his own, from that which he had yesterday, or will have tomorrow. (p. 478, Book III, Chapter VI, vi)

Not only does my understanding of the complex idea of "goodness" differ from yours, my understanding of it will also evolve and change over time. For Locke, words do not facilitate understanding of thoughts and ideas. Rather, they get in the way! It is impossible for us to express our ideas in a pure form. Instead, we are compelled to use the medium of words, which change our ideas into something else which can only approximate what we are thinking.

The meanings of words can be altered by a change of tone in which they are expressed or by the accompaniment of nonverbal behaviors such as a nod, a wink, or a knowing smile. Two people can collapse in fits of laughter at an in-joke while a third has no comprehension of what was funny. There are many potential interpretations of any message available to a receiver, and many ways in which the context and nonverbal accompaniments, quite independent of the message, can cause those interpretations to shift. For Locke, using words to express clear and distinct perceptions is a contradiction in terms.

What is a Poor Communicator to Do?

As we have seen, Locke adopted a skeptical approach to language and communication. It is this type of skepticism that drives much of our contemporary discourses of communication. Since communication is treated as a "problem," the justification for much contemporary interest in communication is that it purports to provide solutions. Since communication is constituted as being *inherently* problematic, i.e., it is a problem that can never be solved because communication is a problematic state by its very nature, there will *always* be a need and a market for those who claim to offer communication solutions. The Lockean discourse of communication makes possible and justifies an entire industry of communication classes, workshops, and training through the articulation of what can be identified as "good communication." Within the transmission regime of communication, the "good communicator" is that person who can encode and transmit messages in way that the idea received is as close as possible to the idea sent. Communication theorist David Berlo (1960) expresses the scenario as follows:

> Given a purpose for communicating, a response which is to be elicited, a communicator hopes that his communication will have fidelity. By fidelity, we mean that he will get what he wants. A high-fidelity encoder is one that expresses the meaning of the source perfectly. A high-fidelity decoder is one that translates a message for the receiver with complete accuracy. In analyzing communication, we are interested in determining what increases or reduces the fidelity of the process. (p. 40)

My students express similar sentiments as Berlo during our discussions of "What is communication?" They often claim that their motivation for taking a course or program in communication is to improve their personal communication skills. Communication practitioners and scholars are ready and able to respond to such a perceived need. Such scholars and practitioners make careers out of identifying communication problems in all kinds of areas: personal relationships, small groups, organizations, international relationships, and so on. Students see the main function of communication teachers as being able to offer solutions, strategies, and appropriate theory to help them deal with the various problems they have so eloquently identified.

Much familiar communication discourse is motivated and shaped by such concerns. For example, communication scholars Stanley Deetz and

Sheryl Stevenson (1986) suggest that there are two basic questions that must be considered in constructing a message: (a) *What* is to be said? and (b) *How* is it to be said? In relating a message to another person, the speaker needs to decide on the content (what) of the message and the process (how) of expression. As Deetz and Stevenson (1986) point out, "adaptation of the message may lead to different content or different processes when the situation is different or different people are present" (p. 34). As John Locke recognized in 1690, there is always the question of *choice* in any communication situation. For Locke, this aspect of choice is a fundamental problem for the philosopher attempting to transit fundamental truths to others since communication and message construction is always contingent on the situation and the participants. Locke is faced with the prospect of communicating an absolute message through a process that is contingent. He is faced with the fact that there is no absolute best or correct way in which to communicate his ideas.

As the author of this book, I am also well aware of this as I write, rewrite, and rewrite again the multiple drafts of this book. I know that even the final draft that you now hold in your hand is capable of improvement. There is always a better turn of phrase, or another reference, or another quote from Locke that could improve and make clearer the text you are reading here. In a sense, this book can never really be finished. It is just a step on the path to something else. Philosopher of science Jacob Bronowski recognized this in the case of the artist painting a portrait of someone's face. Bronowski (1973) writes: "We are aware that these pictures do not so much fix the face as explore it; that the artist is tracing the detail almost as if by touch; and that each line that is added strengthens the picture but never makes it final" (p. 353).

For Locke, the contingent nature of communication was a fundamental problem. However, for modern communication scholars and practitioners, the contingent nature of communication is a blessing! It provides the basis on which they can claim that "expertise in communication" is knowing the best choices to make in constructing messages for any particular situation or person. They can also teach you the principles by which to make those choices. Paramount among these principles is the golden rule of effective communication: *know your audience before you speak.* For example, in his book on communicating effectively through writing, Michael Goodman (1984) notes:

> Think of the person the letter or report goes to, and think of other possible readers as well. Then ask yourself: What is the best way to present this information to the reader? . . . A capable writer

should be able to present the same information in different ways. (p. 4)

In the public speaking situation, Stephen Lucas (1995) makes the importance of knowing the audience clear:

Good speakers are audience centered. They know the primary purpose of speech making is not to display one's learning or demonstrate one's superiority or blow off steam. Rather, it is to gain a *desired response* from listeners. (p. 90)

Lucas (1995, p. 91) offers the following considerations public speakers should take into account when preparing (encoding) their ideas for public presentation:

- To whom am I speaking?
- What do I want them to know, believe, or do as a result of my speech?
- What is the most effective way of composing and presenting my speech to accomplish that aim?

Not only is the content of a message contingent upon the receiver and the situation, the manner in which that message is physically presented is also contingent. There are many ways in which any message can be presented to another person. Again, communication "experts" provide principles and expertise on how to deal with these choices. Speaking as a so-called "communication expert," allow me to refer to my own teaching notes to articulate some of the choices and strategies presented to students as part of a class in public speaking.

Pacing and Pauses: Many novice speakers are nervous about giving a speech. This nervousness can become translated into the speaker rushing the speech. Speakers go through the introduction and main points before the audience has been given a chance to assimilate or even, in some cases, to understand the information being presented. You need to make a conscious effort to slow down, take your time, and not be afraid to scan the audience for feedback to make sure they have grasped the point being made.

Be sure to make appropriate use of pauses. A pause is the time in a speech when the speaker actually stops talking for a moment. Pauses are important because they signal the structure of the speech. They let the audience know when one part of the speech is ending and another is beginning: e.g., between the introduction and the main body, or between main points, or between the main body and the conclusion. They break up the speech as it is delivered in the same way that section headings break it up as it is written.

Eye Contact: Without appropriate eye contact, the most wonderfully structured and well researched speech will be totally ineffective. It is through eye contact that the communicative bond is established between speaker and audience. Communication in public speaking is not just a question of delivery, or visual aids, or fancy language (i.e., things that pertain to the speaker alone), but, at its most fundamental level, a matter of looking at the audience and having them look back at you. Speakers who refuse to establish eye contact are perceived as tentative and ill at ease. At worst, they are perceived as insincere or dishonest.

More important than this, however, is that invariably a lack of eye contact leads to a failure to be flexible because it cuts off feedback communicating the audience's reactions to the speaker. A speaker who ploughs through a speech with little regard for the audience's understanding will cause the audience to become alienated and the speech to lose its impact. Adapting to the audience, therefore, is not just a matter of putting in an appropriate sentence in the speech which says that "you should listen to this because. . ." Good audience adaptation means literally what it says: the speaker must adapt to the audience as she speaks, and all throughout the speech. Not just in terms of what she is saying, but in how it is said. Generally, bad eye contact is correlated with rushed speeches. Good eye contact is correlated with speeches where the speaker is prepared to pause, scan the audience, and adapt on the basis of the feedback they are getting.

Vocal Variety: At various points in the speech, especially in the main body, devices should be introduced to regain the audience periodically. Humor might work for some people, or an example that touches on personal experience, or something surprising. It is important that speeches are not totally predictable. Regarding delivery, variety can be introduced by varying aspects in the rate, volume, and pitch of the voice. Speakers can emphasize main points with pauses or an increase in volume. Vocal variety is an effective way of introducing that touch of unpredictability that will keep the audience with a speaker. One can see the intimate relation that speed, pauses, and eye contact have with the notion of variety. The trick, of course, is knowing precisely when to vary either rate and volume, or when to pause. One cannot explicitly plan this. It can only come with experience and being prepared to read an audience and adapt to it on the spot.

This manner of speaking about communication is instantly recognizable by my students. Indeed, much of it is common sense to them already. Yet, for many, if not most, of the students, this is the knowledge about communication that they want to learn. It is what they *expect* to learn, and they often raise their eyebrows when they are exposed to something different. These expectations are shaped by the unspoken knowledge that communication is intrinsically imperfect and, as such, is *always* capable of improvement. In these beliefs, my students are following the discourse of John Locke written in 1690, and which have now become the basis of our common sense understandings of the nature of communication.

Three
How Communication Became Known as Information Processing:
The True Psychical Reality

The unconscious is the true psychical reality; in its innermost nature it is as much unknown to us as the reality of the external world, and it is as incompletely presented by the data of consciousness as is the external world by the communications of our sense organs. (Sigmund Freud)

One reason why my students get so frustrated in our discussions of "What is communication?" is that we always arrive, sooner or later, at the notion of the unconscious.

My students like to say things like "a receiver hears my words and, through a process of interpretation, derives my meaning."

"Where does this act of interpretation take place?" I ask. "Can you introspect and feel your mind interpreting these words as I speak them?"

After an attempt at introspection, the students are quick to admit that they cannot experience the process by which they interpret my words. They are aware of ideas they have, at least in the sense that they are aware of having an internal dialogue with themselves, but they cannot make themselves aware of how this inner dialogue is produced.

Wittgenstein (1958) would liken my students' problem to trying to see the location of our visual sense. I can say something like "I see a cat in the middle of my visual field." But wherein can you see the visual field *itself*? Similarly, I can close my eyes and report to you that I am experiencing a thought about my daughter's pet cat, Lucifer. I can experience my thought of the cat, but how can I experience the act of thinking? However, my students' allegiance to the regime of communication means that they do not then go on to conclude that such processes do not exist. That would be the equivalent of Leonard Shelby closing his eyes and believing the world ceases to exist just because he cannot see it. Just because my students cannot experience the process of thinking in itself does not mean they believe that such processes are not real. The students proceed to argue, quite sensibly, that these mental processes must therefore take place somewhere beyond their capacity to be aware of them. And they have a word for such a place: the unconscious.

Students are quite happy to talk about the unconscious. All kinds of things take place there. For example, the students tell me that memories are stored in the unconscious until they choose to retrieve them or until they are activated by some external stimulation. So you see the face of a person you have not seen in a long time, and their name is automatically retrieved from your memory and associated with the face. You become aware of the name, even though you are not aware of the mental process through which the name was searched for, located, and retrieved. That mechanism is, as my students explain, unconscious. Further, my students tell me that their memories *must* be stored unconsciously since they are not aware of all of their memories all of the time. That would result in mental chaos.

I ask the students to describe for me the experience of their unconscious mind locating and retrieving specific memories; something they did the day before, perhaps. At this point, the students are quite happy to tell me that they cannot do this, of course, precisely because such a process is unconscious! Some smile and claim to have won the argument at this point. With the invocation of an unconscious process, the world of communication quickly falls back into focus again. In this spirit, ideas, thoughts, and meaning are all spoken of as epi-phenomena. The mechanics of the deeper reality behind these appearances (the production, the interpretation, the storing) takes place in the unconscious.

My students are not alone nor indeed unusual in advocating this viewpoint. Indeed, I am the one who is accused of being unusual by daring to question it. Their description of the place of an unconscious in their understanding of communication is not a theory that they made up spontaneously. Again, the students quickly form a solid consensus around its main tenets. The role of the unconscious is a central part of the regime that structures their discourse about communication. It follows neatly from their Lockean conception of mind and ideas because it provides a place for the activities of the human understanding to take place (the interpretation of stimuli, the reflection and connections necessary for the construction of complex ideas, the assignment of words to ideas, and so on).

It is also part of a prevailing way of talking about the mind that goes back to the seminal discourse of experimental psychology that took place in the late nineteenth century and early twentieth century. The transformation of psychology into a science *required* the invocation of a domain like the unconscious. It was to be the place where the truth could be found-the reality beyond the surface appearance. As we shall see, this discourse was to have a profound impact on contemporary discourse concerning communication.

A Philosophy of the Unconscious

Mankind very naturally began its researches in Philosophy with the examination of what was immediately given in Consciousness; may it not now be lured, by the charm of novelty and the hope of a great reward, to seek the golden treasure in the mountain's depths, in the noble ores of its rocky beds, rather than on the surface of the fruitful earth? (Eduard von Hartmann)

The sense in which my students use the term "unconscious" is a nineteenth century development (Williams, 1983). In its most literal sense, to be "unconscious" is to be without consciousness, as in a sentence such as

"The boxer was knocked unconscious."

In the development of nineteenth century psychology, however, the use of the word shifted from a dynamic process of someone or something (a dream, a memory) *becoming* unconscious to the creation of a primary and autonomous "unconscious mind." As Williams (1983) explains, in this conception, the unconscious is taken "not only as being stronger than **conscious** mental or emotional activity, but as its true (if ordinarily hidden) source" (p. 322). Consider the impact of the work of the nineteenth century German philosopher, Eduard von Hartmann, and his influential work

Philosophy of the Unconscious (Hartmann, 1884/1931). In his introduction, Hartmann wrote:

> The sphere of Consciousness is like a vine-clad hill which has so often been ploughed up in all directions, that the thought of further labour has become almost loathsome to the public mind; for the looked-for treasure is never found, although rich and unexpected crops have sprung from the well-worked soil. Mankind very naturally began its researches in Philosophy with the examination of what was immediately given in Consciousness; may it not now be lured, by the charm of novelty and the hope of a great reward, to seek the golden treasure in the mountain's depths, in the noble ores of its rocky beds, rather than on the surface of the fruitful earth? (p. 2)

Hartmann is expressing the view that the reality of the human being *lies beneath* what can be immediately experienced in consciousness, much like my students argue that their ability to communicate must somehow be explained by a process that lies *behind* their communicative acts, such as the thought or the idea. My students, like Hartmann, recognize that there is "something more" behind the communicative act from which it springs and by which it is made possible. *Behind* the word is the meaning. *Behind* the meaning is the idea. *Behind* the idea is the conscious mind. *Behind* the conscious mind is the realm of the unconscious mind. Hartmann argues that we can no longer be content with the study of consciousness. We need to go beyond consciousness to explore that which makes consciousness possible. As Hartmann (1884/1931) states, should we not "seek the golden treasure in the mountain's depths, in the noble ores of its rocky beds, rather than on the surface of the fruitful earth?" (p. 2).

The prospect of discovering golden treasure in the unconscious created something of an intellectual gold rush at the beginning of the twentieth century. American psychologist G. Stanley Hall hailed Hartmann's work as being the equivalent of a Copernican revolution, alongside such names as Galileo, Sir Isaac Newton, Immanuel Kant, and Albert Einstein. Hall (1912) wrote that Hartmann's

> Proof of the eccentric, penumbral, peripheral, marginal nature of consciousness makes him a modern Copernicus. The erection of the Unconscious as a world principle marks the great revolution of views since the Renaissance, which was its prelude, in emancipating the world from the views of the past. (p. 238)

39

Hartmann published the *Philosophy of the Unconscious* in Germany in 1884 when he was twenty-two years of age. At the time of its publication, Hartmann was hailed as "the founder of the latest, and at present the most popular Philosophy of the Absolute" (Bowen, 1889, p. 429). Hall (1912) suggested that Hartmann was unquestionably "the most conspicuous figure in the philosophical world for years" (p. 181) and included him among his six "founders of modern psychology," along with Wilhelm Wundt, Hermann Helmholtz, and Gustave Fechner. Bowen (1889) noted that "the work had immediate and great success . . . the book in eight years passed through seven successive editions, and raised a hailstorm of review articles and pamphlets. This remarkable success was fully deserved" (p. 431). Saltus (1885) observed that the *Philosophy of the Unconscious* is "very generally considered as the chief philosophical event of the last two decades" (p. 166). Darnoi (1967) writes that "the unexpected triumph of the work and the universal acclaim of its author . . . established young von Hartmann among the literary notables of the day and launched him on a career that lasted for forty-two years" (p. 12) and that:

> The best known critics of the day, Gottschall, Carriere, Lorm, and Scherr, hailed the young author and his work as the beginning of a new era in philosophical literature, and recommended it enthusiastically to their readers. The copies of the first publication disappeared from the bookstores within a few months. Foreign countries hurried to obtain copyrights for translation. The universities of Leipzig and Gottingen offered him chairs of philosophy, and the Prussian Ministry of Culture invited him to the University of Berlin. (p. 12)

By the last decade of the nineteenth century, the concept of the unconscious was so widespread in Germany and Britain, and to a lesser extent in France, that by then the existence of the unconscious mind had become a common assumption of educated and psychological discussions. A sequence of German thinkers made the idea of the unconscious commonplace by 1880: Arthur Schopenhaeur, Gustav Fechner, Eduard von Hartmann, and Frederick Nietzsche. This time period is marked by the emergence of many seminal texts in the foundation of modern psychological discourse, all of which placed a concept of the unconscious at the center of their thinking. These include Gustav Fechner's (1860/1966) psychophysics, Sigmund Freud's (1900/1965) *The Interpretation of Dreams*, William James's (1890/1950) articulation of his *Principles of Psychology*, the founding of the Society for Psychical Research in England and the American

Society for Psychical Research in the United States (Gauld, 1968), and the Frederick Myers's coining of the term "subliminal consciousness" (Myers, 1891/1976).

The profound impact of the unconscious in the late nineteenth century and early twentieth century has been largely forgotten today. But the logic of this discourse, and the power of the golden treasure metaphor, remains a dominant component of modern transmission views of communication. Because they follow a Lockean logic, modern ways of talking about communication also require a discourse for talking about the mind. When students articulate their understanding of the term "communication," they are also articulating their understanding of how ideas are encoded and decoded within peoples' minds. The invocation of the unconscious is an important part of this explanation. However, the importance of the unconscious lies less in its invocation as a place or a mechanism. Like the conduit metaphor which shapes modern discourses of communication, the unconscious is extremely useful as a discursive strategy. It's not as if my students believe in the unconscious in any whole hearted way. They are at a loss to explain where it is or how it works. Rather, invoking the unconscious enables my students to "go somewhere" when I persist in my questions to them. It provides a limit where we can argue no further.

The unconscious would come to play the same or similar roles in the scientific exploration and explanation of the mind. This is why Hartmann's work was lauded in Copernican terms at the end of the nineteenth century. Hall argued that Hartmann had offered a radically new way of talking about the human mind that made it amenable to scientific discourse. Copernicus replaced the Earth with the Sun at the center of his solar system in a way that enabled accurate measurement and prediction of planetary motion. Hartmann's foregrounding of that which lay behind consciousness would do the same for the fledgling discipline of modern psychology and, ultimately, for our contemporary regime of communication.

Speaking Scientifically about Inner Experience

On the horizon of any human science, there is the project of bringing man's consciousness back to its real conditions, of restoring it to the contents and forms that brought it into being, and elude us within it; this is why the problem of the unconscious-its possibility, status, mode of existence, the means of knowing it and of bringing it to light-is not simply a problem within the human sciences which they can be thought of as

41

> *encountering by chance in their steps; it is a problem that is*
> *ultimately coextensive with their very existence. (Michel*
> *Foucault)*

The struggle of my students' attempts to articulate a coherent and empirical discourse of communication is also clearly seen in the struggles faced by early experimental psychologists to develop a program of empirical research into unconscious mental processes. In the late nineteenth century, interest in psychology was driven by the desire to understand *covert* influences on a person's behavior. Such influences included such things as a person's wishes, plans, motives, traits, perceptions, memories, emotions, feelings, and instincts, and the physiological substrates of these (Richards, 1992). The goal of the empirical psychologist was to evaluate and generate theories of "the psychological" according to prevailing criteria of scientific theory construction and testing. In order to be considered a *bona fide* scientific enterprise, and to obtain the intellectual legitimacy such recognition would bring, it was essential that this subject matter be accorded the same ontological status as the subject matters of other scientific disciplines: i.e., "the psychological" really exists as a natural object for this inquiry. It is against this backdrop that our current discourses concerning communication have been framed.

We can see this move to situate the unconscious as the foundation of an empirical and scientific account of the mind in the writings of the so-called founding fathers of modern psychology. Consider the work of Wilhelm Wundt, who is credited by the *Oxford Companion to the Mind* as being the "father of experimental psychology" (Gregory, 1987, p. 816). Wundt's most important book, *Grundzuge der Physiologische Psychologie*, was first published in 1873-74 and went into six editions. It presented psychology as an independent scientific discipline complementary to anatomy and physiology, but in no sense reducible to them. In his articulation of "the psychological," Wundt (1896) claimed the object of an experimental science of psychology to be inner experience: "Man himself, not as he appears from without, but as he is in his own immediate experience, is the real problem of psychology" (p. 7).

Wundt (1896) advocated that the experimental psychologist does not begin with conscious experience, but rather with objective facts which are empirically available to the scientist:

> Be it sensation, feeling, idea, and will which led in the first instance to the assumption of mind, the only natural method of psychological investigation will be that which begins with just

these facts. First of all we must understand their empirical nature, and then go on to reflect upon them. For it is experience and reflection which constitute each and every science. Experience comes first; it gives us our bricks: reflection is the mortar, which holds the bricks together. We cannot build without both. (p. 8)

Wundt is expressing a view very similar to the empirical philosophy of John Locke, and this connection will further strengthen the place of a psychological base for our contemporary discourses of communication. Wundt's assertion that "experience comes first; it gives us our bricks: reflection is the mortar, which holds the bricks together" mirrors Locke's distinctions between simple and complex ideas. Wundt attempts to develop a methodology from these propositions which can describe the mind using observable facts rather than the self-reports of subjects. As the experience of my students makes clear, it is a waste of time asking people to try and experience the process of *having* a thought (as opposed to the content of that thought). As a consequence, it is necessary to go beyond subjective and unreliable self-reports and look directly at those empirical processes that make such reports possible.

For Wundt, like Locke, the basic unit for describing these processes will be the empirically observable and measurable unit of sensation. Sensation is a fact of experience, not a product of self-introspection, that exists in the world. The experimental psychologist, like Locke, must approach them without presupposition and observe, record, and reflect on these objective events. It is only on the basis of this empirical turn that modern psychology can claim to be scientific.

With the adoption of this natural science standpoint, the *facts* of modern psychology are established by implication. For Wundt (1896), such facts include "sensation, feeling, idea, and will" (p. 8). Any legitimate psychological phenomena have to be consistent with the self evident facts the psychologist seeks to describe. This places fundamental limits on the type of acceptable statement that can be made about psychological phenomena. Within this framework, the major issue for the early modern psychologists was: How can one measure the self-evident facts of sensation, feeling, idea, and will? In pursuing this question, the operationalization of these constructs produced their definition. For example, the meaning of the term "sensation" was derived from the operations performed in its demonstration and measurement.

The object of study for early psychologists was not the mind directly, but rather the description of patterns and correlations of external stimulation.

From the observation of external stimulation and responses, the operations of the mind are *inferred* rather than observed. As Wundt (1896) explains:

> In psychology we find that only those mental phenomena which are directly accessible to physical influences can be made the subject matter of experiment. We cannot experiment upon mind itself, but only upon its outworks, the organs of sense and movement which are functionally related to mental processes. (p. 10)

Trying to create legitimate inferences from these correlations is an enormous task. It can be likened to a person sitting outside of a library who observes and records patrons entering with certain books and leaving with certain books. Given the patterns and correlations between the books entering and leaving the library, the observer must somehow infer the cataloguing system by which the books are organized in the library.

By adopting the natural science approach to the study of inner experience, modern psychology is forced to constitute knowledge in terms of phenomena *different* from the internal experience of the subject. Instead, priority is given to a consideration of the organs of sense and their empirical relationships with external stimulation. Although Wundt (1896) explicitly claims modern psychology to be the science of "internal experience," in the experimental context the subject is treated as a *performer* rather than a person who experiences. Subjects of psychological experiments are viewed in terms how quickly they can react, how accurately they can perceive, and how completely they can recall. Conclusions about the subject's "internal experience" are drawn by the psychologist, not the subject, since to report what one feels is subjective and therefore prone to error beyond the experimenter's control. The objective of the psychologist is to *see through* the reported experience of the individual to get at *what is really happening*. As Wundt (1896) asserts:

> If we try to observe our mental activities, the observer and the observed object are one and the same. But the most important condition of a trustworthy observation is always thought to consist in the mutual independence of object and observer. (p. 12)

In order to be considered scientific, modern psychology must create a *fundamental split* between the experience to be explained and the person who experiences that experience. The experiencer in whose experience the psychologist is interested must be taken out of the domain of relevant objects of knowledge since their direct observations are not trustworthy. Of paramount importance is the indirect observation of the psychologist and the manipulation of stimuli; that which lies outside of the experiencer, which nevertheless are assumed to give rise to the experience that is being experienced. As Wundt (1896) claims:

> We must endeavour so to control our mental processes by means of objective stimulation of the external organs (particularly of the sense-organs, with the physiological functioning of which definite psychoses are regularly connected) that the disturbing influence which the condition of observation tends to exercise upon them is counteracted. (p. 13)

Not only is the experiencer of one's own experience to be systematically excluded from the discourse of modern psychology, she is also considered to be a "disturbing influence" which has to be actively "counteracted" by the methodology of the psychologist. Modern psychology bypasses the subject as subject in order to explain the subject as object. Consciousness and experience do not represent objects in themselves, but instead are considered as the end result of a composite of objective elements such as sensation. It is in these empirical relationships between objective elements that the golden treasure is to be inferred. As Wundt (1896) claims:

> An idea . . . is always something composite. . . . Our first problem in analyzing ideas, therefore, consists in the determination of their simplest constituent elements, and in the investigation of the psychological properties of these. We call the psychological elements of ideas Sensations. (pp. 14-15)

In other words, to understand ideas, it is necessary to understand something other than ideas, since an idea is always composed of something else. Modern psychology demands the reduction of phenomenon to fact, fact being understood as being something other than experience. It is not something which lies outside of experience, as if the two comprised two separate realms, but rather that the facts of sensation constitute and comprise experience. Such facts are themselves totally devoid of consciousness and human self-hood. This idea is described by Munsterberg (1910) as follows:

> Psychology considers the inner experience . . . for its special purpose as a series of describable phenomena; it transforms the

> felt realities of will into perceivable objects, into contents of consciousness. Through this transformation the real purposiveness, yes, the whole inner connection of the will act is eliminated; the psychological phenomena as such have no intentions and no significance any more but are merely bits of lifeless mental material, complexes of unphysical objects made up of elements which we call sensations. (pp. 26-27)

The idea of a "science of human consciousness" is therefore contradictory in its very formulation. Psychology, conceived as a natural science, is faced with the apparently absurd and self-contradictory task of investigating consciousness as part of the realm of things. This is self-contradictory because the realm of things is what *appears to* consciousness, or what exists independently of consciousness. As Giorgi (1970) explains the problem, "psychology must strip consciousness of consciousness in order to investigate consciousness scientifically" (p. 74). This description of consciousness through the investigation of elements that are nonconscious is the problem that the discourse of modern psychology has set itself up to resolve. It must investigate consciousness as an object in the world that is independent of consciousness.

The account of the human individual in terms of something other than what is conscious demands the introduction of a third component; the limen, the threshold at which nonconscious mental processes become the realm of consciousness that one knows in experience. The limen is the point at which the object becomes subject and when objective process becomes subjective experience. It also provides the criterion by which the psychologist can differentiate between the objective and the subjective. The discourse of modern psychology demands the investigation of the limen and the empirical differentiation of the supraliminal, that which lies above the limen (consciousness, awareness, subjective experience), from the subliminal, that which lies below the limen (the unconscious, objective inner experience). This distinction is demonstrated in the following statement by William James (1902/1958):

> The subliminal region, whatever else it may be, is at any rate a place now admitted by psychologists to exist for the accumulation of vestiges of sensible experience (whether inattentively or attentively registered), and for their elaboration according to ordinary psychological or logical laws into results that end by attaining such a "tension" that they may at times enter consciousness with something like a burst. It thus is "scientific"

to interpret all otherwise unaccountable invasive alterations of consciousness as results of the tension of subliminal memories reaching the bursting point. (p. 188)

The term "limen" here does not refer to the threshold between two states, as if there were two objects of conscious and unconscious that this limen separated. It does not mean that this limen is real, and that real entities exist above and below it. The appearance of the term "limen" represents the difference between what can be talked about scientifically and what cannot when it comes to the scientific description of the human individual. The limen is a construction which operates to demarcate statements about truth. It allows the psychologist to demonstrate that she is not talking about subjective consciousness, but objective unconsciousness. One is not talking about what the subject feels, but what constitutes feeling. The truth of the human individual lies not in what is experienced, but in what cannot be experienced, of that which constitutes experience and yet, at the same time, eludes it.

The problem of the threshold was a foundational and constitutive problematic of the fledgling discipline of modern psychology. Fechner's (1860/1966) psychophysics, claimed by modern histories to be the prototype of modern experimental psychology, was exclusively concerned with the measurement of thresholds. James (1902/1958) called the introduction of the limen into the discourse of modern psychology to be the most important step forward in the scientific description of the human individual:

I cannot but think that the most important step forward that has occurred in psychology since I have been a student of that science is the discovery, first made in 1886, that in certain subjects at least, there is not only the consciousness of the ordinary field, with its usual center and margin, but an addition thereto in the shape of a set of memories, thoughts, and feelings which are extra-marginal and outside of the primary consciousness altogether, but yet must be classed as conscious facts of some sort, able to reveal their presence by unmistakable signs. I call this the most important step forward because, unlike the other advances which psychology has made, this discovery has revealed to us an entirely unsuspected peculiarity in the constitution of human nature. No other step forward which psychology has made can proffer any such claim as this. (p. 188)

The problem of the unconscious, the marginal, and the subconscious represents a distinct realm of investigation where science can locate its statements concerning the truth. Lipps (1897) proclaimed that the problem of the unconscious in modern psychology is less *a* psychological problem than *the* problem of psychology (quoted in Freud, 1900/1965, p. 650). Freud (1900/1965) also argued that:

> The unconscious is the true psychical reality; *in its innermost nature it is as much unknown to us as the reality of the external world, and it is as incompletely presented by the data of consciousness as is the external world by the communications of our sense organs.* (p. 651, emphasis in original)

Finally, Bergson (1913) asserted that:

> To explore the most sacred depths of the unconscious, to labor in what I have just called the subsoil of consciousness, that will be the principal task of psychology in the century which is opening. (quoted in Prince, 1921, p. viii)

Michel Foucault has argued that the unconscious, that which is unthought, represents the very foundations upon which any scientific description of the human individual is made possible. This includes, as we shall see, our contemporary discourses of communication. Without the unthought, the scientific description of Wundt's inner experience would be impossible. As Foucault (1966/1973) points out:

> On the horizon of any human science, there is the project of bringing man's consciousness back to its real conditions, of restoring it to the contents and forms that brought it into being, and elude us within it; this is why the problem of the unconscious-its possibility, status, mode of existence, the means of knowing it and of bringing it to light-is not simply a problem within the human sciences which they can be thought of as encountering by chance in their steps; it is a problem that is ultimately coextensive with their very existence. A transcendental raising of level that is, on the other side, an unveiling of the non-conscious is constitutive of all the sciences of man. (p. 364)

The unthought represents the conditions of possibility for any human science. Modern psychology is only one possible discourse that laid claim to the title of science of the unconscious (see Bradby, 1920; Fuller, 1986; Hartmann, 1884/1931; Klein, 1979; Munsterberg, Ribot, Janet, Jastrow, Hart, and Prince, 1910; Northridge, 1924; Prince, 1921; Waldstein, 1894/1926; Whyte, 1960/1978). The conscious/unconscious dichotomy provided the conditions of possibility for a science of psychical phenomena which was very active at the turn of the twentieth century (Gauld, 1968; Lodge, 1909; Myers, 1891/1976; Shepard, 1985). This system of knowledge claims constituted disassociated states as being synthesized into a large self-conscious personality. The mind of a person consists of two quite distinct realms, both of which are "conscious" but only one of which is conscious to the individual. As Myers (1891/1976) describes:

> The stream of consciousness in which we habitually live is not the only consciousness which exists in connection with our organism. Our habitual or empirical consciousness may consist of a mere selection from a multitude of thoughts and sensations, of which some at least are equally conscious with those that we empirically know. (p. 301)

In a letter to James Sully dated March 3, 1901, William James wrote: "I seriously believe that the general problem of the subliminal, as Myers propounds it, promises to be one of the *great* problems, possibly even the greatest problem, of psychology" (Murphy & Ballou, 1973, p. 69).

The appearance of Freud's (1900/1965) discourse of the unconscious at this time is also made possible by this fundamental dichotomy and the location of an objective domain through which the actions and experiences of a human individual could be described. Freud invoked the unconscious realm in terms of disassociated or split-off ideas. These ideas were active, although the subject was not aware of them. Freud's (1900/1965) examination on dreams explicitly claimed to be scientific on the grounds that it sought to describe the working of the unconscious mechanisms by which consciousness is constituted. Freud referred to such a domain as the operation of a "*mental* apparatus built up of a number of agencies arranged in a series one behind the other" (p. 81). The analysis of dreams was seen as a phenomena at which the limen from mental apparatus and conscious awareness is at its most visible. Freud (1900/1965) argued that dreams were not "the mere lowering of conscious mental life below the main threshold" (p. 81). They were a reflection of the apparatus that operated without awareness, and the dream was a tool by which one could describe its agencies.

Communication as Information Processing

The task of the psychologist trying to understand human cognition is analogous to that of a man trying to discover how a computer has been programmed. In particular, if the program seems to store and reuse information, he would like to know by what "routines" or "procedures" this is done. (Ulric Neisser)

The discussions I have with my students about "What is communication?" are always structured around a particular discourse concerning the nature of people. What they describe to me is not only how they see communication, but how they see themselves as human beings. The students' accounts almost always involve describing themselves as machines. The unconscious is that place where all the machinery works. Inside their heads, processes move and spin to produce thoughts, ideas, and memory. Mechanisms of perception take in and make sense of incoming stimuli. Master routines generate appropriate outputs and behavior. Communication is described as a product of their mental machinery. It is an output made possible by an underlying system of routines and processes which lie beyond their conscious awareness, but which still nevertheless exist for them. What my students are describing, whether they know it or not, is a view of the human individual as a processor of information.

The information processing paradigm in modern cognitive psychology is explicitly based on a computer metaphor (see Loftus & Schooler, 1985). The computer introduced a new set of linguistic resources with which an unconscious foundation for human action could be described. The technological advances in computing technology that took place during the Second World War made it possible to talk materialistically about mental concepts that had previously been considered beyond the means of scientific description and investigation. As psychologist George Miller (1983) explains, "the engineers showed us how to build a machine that has memory, a machine that has purpose, a machine that plays chess . . . and so on. If they can do that, then the kind of things they say about machines, a psychologist should be permitted to say about a human being" (p. 23).

Hunt (1982) points out that the computer metaphor does not refer to hardware aspects, i.e., the comparison of the brain with computer circuitry. Rather, "what does work as a metaphor is a somewhat computer like 'set of transformations' of information from the moment of perception on" (p. 101). The new principles and insights derived from computer science offered a scientific vocabulary for describing mental states. This enabled the discourse of the human individual as information processor to come into being. According to Ulric Neisser (1967):

> The task of the psychologist trying to understand human cognition is analogous to that of a man trying to discover how a computer has been programmed. In particular, if the program seems to store and reuse information, he would like to know by what "routines" or "procedures" this is done. (p. 6)

Within the context of a psychological discourse derived from computer metaphors, the principal task engaged in by human beings is not some vague notion of "thinking," but a rigorous and operationalizable notion of information processing. From this perspective, "a person is seen as constantly taking in information from the environment and then storing, manipulating, and recoding portions of this information in a succession of memory stages" (Loftus & Loftus, 1976, p. xi). A computer receives input and, by a series of logically programmed transformations, produces a useful answer. A human information processing system is conceptualized in a similar way. A person takes in raw stimuli from the environment, processes it via a series of logical stages, and produces a meaningful response on the basis of that processing. The task of the psychologist is to describe and understand the nature of these various internal stages. The psychologist seeks to explain the nature of the program which acts upon the data.

This way of talking about human cognition has a number of important connections with Locke's view of communication. For example, a person's communicative behavior is not a direct response to the world around her. Rather, communication is the end result of the operations of a cognitive system which has processed incoming information from the senses. A person has no direct contact with the real world at all. She can only experience the world that is created for her by her perceptual and cognitive systems. This idea is not a new insight by any means. Immanuel Kant (1781/1965) argued in his *Critique of Pure Reason* that you can never experience things in themselves. Relax for a moment and consider the experience you are having right now as you hold this book in front of your face. As you examine the words on this page, are you seeing the book "as it is"? Or are you seeing something else, a "creation" of your mind built from a constant stream of meaningless stimulation (light energy, for example) that enters through your senses? Kant argued that you can never see "outside" of yourself. Everything you will ever know through the having of experience is only a knowledge of your own mental states. The task of the psychologist is made possible by the realization that there is and must be something making it possible for you to have experiences such as the one you are having right now looking at this book. Expressed in terms of information processing, Geoffrey Underwood (1978) makes the point as follows:

> The world we experience is the world as it was rather than the world as it is. The reality which we experience is quite artificial . . ., for the world of which we are conscious is the product of a series of processes applied to sensory data over a period of time (p. 9).

Given that these processes *must* exist, what is the nature of these processes? How do they work? And how is an understanding of these processes related to the regime of communication articulated by my students?

Cognitive psychologists speak of three major stages in which the processing of incoming sensory stimulation takes place. The first of these processes is *sensory memory*; the initial point of contact between the information processing system and the environment. The amount of information available to the system from the environment is limited only by the capacity of the sensory apparatus that receives the stimulation. However, the amount of potential information that could be made available for processing is enormous. Therefore the information processing system must *select* pertinent information for further processing and screen out information that is not pertinent. Such initial selection is based on criteria such as relevance to system goals, biological need, and danger (Dixon 1981). Sensory memory is extremely brief, certainly no more than one second, and is the first stage in the system where selection can take place. Its function is to hold raw and essentially meaningless stimulation streaming in from the environment long enough for a very rudimentary analysis and selection procedure to be performed. Information not selected for further processing is presumed to be lost to the system.

Features of the raw data selected for further processing are passed along to *short-term memory*, which consists of everything you are experiencing right now and has often been equated with the notion of consciousness. Short term memory accepts sensory data from the sense and makes sense of it with respect to information from long-term memory. Our experience of being conscious consists of this constant interplay between short- and long-term memory accepting and making sense of sensory data.

Long-term memory is that store of experience and knowledge that enable us to make sense of a potentially chaotic and random environment. It enables us to order the world into categories, such that we can recognize each new situation as a class of something and not a totally unique experience. This function of long term memory is referred to as *semantic memory* (Tulving, 1972) and comprises our "knowledge of the world"; our categories for knowing what things mean. Semantic memory is composed of *concepts*. For example, the labels "cup," "chair," or "dog" are all concepts which enable us to recognize and make sense of certain physical objects we may encounter in the environment. Although each individual manifestation of a cup is a unique object giving off unique data, we still recognize and understand it as a "cup," even though we may have never seen this particular cup before. Our concepts enable us to know what "people" are, or "trees," "birds," or "computers."

This basic three-stage model has been driving cognitive psychology research since the 1940s. When we take the model and its assumptions as given, we can generate research questions such as:

- How much information can be stored in short-term memory?

- How is that information stored, coded, and processed?

- How is information selected from sensory memory for further processing?

- How is information stored in long-term memory?

- What activates the relevant information in long-term memory to process incoming sensory data?

If one looks beyond the technical language, it becomes clear that these questions look remarkably like communication questions. They essentially ask:

- How does a sender store and access information needed to construct a message?

- How does a receiver process and make sense of information transmitted to her by a sender?

In short,

- What happens inside our heads that makes communication happen?

The earliest studies to use the information processing model were investigations into the phenomenon of attention. These studies are informative in identifying the contours of the language used by my students in their descriptions of communication. Attention addresses the observation that we cannot fully appreciate all that takes place at any one time. For example, at this moment, you, the reader, are concentrating on reading this book. These words and your interpretation of what they mean are presently forming the focus of your attention. The surrounding noise in your immediate environment (the conversation your friends are having in the next room, the hum of the air conditioning unit, the lull of the traffic noise outside of your window) fades from your immediate consciousness. If someone mentions your name in the other room, your attention is very likely to shift from this book to the source of that remark. But no matter how you try, you cannot attend to this book and the conversation of your friend at the same time. Only one of these can claim your attention at any particular moment. The same is true of those students of mine who insist on doing their homework with music playing in the background. They can study their textbook or listen to the lyrics of their Pink Floyd CD, but they cannot do both. While I was writing this book, one of my greatest comforts was repeatedly playing my complete collection of Peter Gabriel CDs on my computer CD player. I knew that when a CD had finished playing, it would be time to stand up and stretch my poor long-suffering back. Yet on many occasions, I didn't even realize that CD had finished playing until much later. I certainly had no recollection of any particular song.

The most famous example of selective attention is the "cocktail party phenomenon" as described by Colin Cherry (1953). The situation he describes is a communication situation. Imagine yourself standing with your friends at a cocktail party (remember, this example was offered by an academic writing in 1953). You are sipping your cocktail and enjoying a conversation with your friend. Around you, the sound of dance music and the chatter of other conversations fills the environment. Cherry wants to know how it is possible that we are able to select the one voice that interests us from the many voices which surround us. The very fact that we *can* hold a conversation in such a noisy setting strongly implies that there *must* be some underlying mental mechanism for screening and selecting sensory input. Donald Broadbent (1958) proposed that the nervous system acts to some extent as a single communication channel and that it is meaningful to regard it as having a limited capacity. The system contains a "selective filter" which can be "tuned" to accept a desired message and "reject" all others. The selection is not completely random. The probability of a particular class of events being selected is increased by certain properties of the events (such as a person saying your name) and certain states of the organism (such as hunger or fatigue). Interestingly, the book in which Broadbent presented his filter thesis was entitled *Perception and Communication.* However, when Broadbent uses the term "communication" in this title, he does not mean communication *between* people. Rather, he considers communication in terms of the passage of information through the stages of his filter model, from when it enters the channel through the senses and exits as it passes from the limited capacity channel into storage.

The point is that everything about perception and attention takes place *inside* the dark place of a person's head. It is the same place that my students locate the reality of communication. It is that place where ideas are "formed" in the mind of a sender. It is that place where ideas are "received," "decoded," and "interpreted" by a receiver. Yet even though Cherry's cocktail party phenomenon represents a familiar communication situation, attention research does not seek to explain communication. Rather attention researchers use our ability to communicate (to distinguish meaningful from non-meaningful symbols, for example) as a means by which to explore how an internal filter mechanism is able to screen out or select particular information streams from the environment. Why is that your attention switches when you hear your name mentioned in the other room, but it doesn't switch when the name mentioned is that of someone who you do not know? How does your personal interest in the subject matter of a message relate to your ability to focus and attend to it? Do you attend more diligently to male or female voices? English of American accents? Messages with rational or emotional appeals? Characteristics such as these are manipulated by experimental psychologists to see what effect they have on a person's ability to attend to and retain a message. But these communication variables are considered interesting not in terms of what they tell us about communication as a phenomenon, but rather what such variables can tell us about the workings of an internal attention mechanism. Indeed, the precursors of modern communication research in the 1950s and 1960s were not concerned with communication at all. Early so-called "communication research" was carried out with the explicit aim of developing an account of information processing within the mind. For example, consider the seminal work of Carl Hovland, who is identified as one of the founding fathers of communication study (see Rogers, 1986). In their introduction to their influential book *Communication and Persuasion,* Hovland, Janis, and Kelley (1953) write:

> While research on communication and persuasion is of considerable practical concern, perhaps its greatest attraction for

the scientist is that it involves central theoretical problems in individual and social psychology. Study of the way in which opinions and beliefs are affected by communication symbols provides an excellent means for examining the role of higher mental processes in assimilating the numerous and often contradictory influences impinging upon the individual in everyday life. (pp. 1-2)

This psychological discourse of communication specifies a particular relationship between mind and communication. Psychology uses communication as a means of describing and understanding the nature of the mind. It does not employ a description of the mind to articulate an understanding of communication. Like the philosophy of Locke in 1690, an understanding of communication is completely secondary to the primary task of addressing the nature of the mind that produced the communication. And yet psychological discourse remains that discourse that dominates the talk of my students and is one reason why the description of communication in these terms is so difficult for them. Almost without exception, the students become compelled to talk about communication in terms of ideas, thoughts, processes of encoding and decoding, all of which are said to occur *inside* their minds. We can see this orientation articulated in the remarks of the American pragmatist philosopher John Dewey back in 1929 when he described the relationship of language and mind in the following way:

Empirical thinkers have rarely ventured in discussion of language beyond reference to some peculiarity of brain structure, or to some psychic peculiarity, such as a tendency to "outer expression" of "inner" states. (Dewey, 1929/1958, p. 169)

Dewey's statement reflects my students' claims that communication is a manifestation of brain function. The brain does something, and then we communicate *as a result*. This view of communication squares cleanly with the role of the unconscious and the nature of scientific legitimation of empirical psychology. Wundt (1896) proposed that to explain the truth of conscious experience it is necessary look beyond consciousness. Similarly, to understand communication, we must look *beyond* communication to something else. This "something else" is inherently psychological in nature. Dewey (1929/1958) expresses the situation as follows:

Social interaction and institutions have been treated as products of a ready-made *specific* physical or mental endowment of a self-

56

sufficing individual, wherein language acts as a mechanical go-between to convey observations and ideas that have prior and independent existence. (p. 169)

The truth of communication lies not in messages or even of behavior, but in the *specific* physical or mental endowment of a self-sufficing individual. Communication merely acts as a conduit to move around independent ideas created by an objective mental process.

When one adopts this psychological view of communication, significant consequences arise for the manner in which communication is talked about and investigated. Communication is made to stand in a particular relationship with mental states. Hence the study of communication also stands in a particular relationship with the discipline of cognitive psychology. Using Dewey's terminology, psychology takes as its domain the "specific physical or mental endowment of a self-sufficing individual" (Dewey, 1929/1958, p. 169), or, in other words, the abilities of the human individual to think, perceive, and act on information derived from the environment and from memory. Communication studies, on the other hand, is left to address the characteristics of the "mechanical go-between" (Dewey, 1929/1958, p. 169) which must presuppose the presence of at least two such individuals between whom an act of communication can take place. Whereas cognitive psychology problematizes the processes by which an action is produced by an individual, communication focuses upon the process through which interaction is made possible and maintained. Thus, communication becomes a "tendency to 'outer expression' of 'inner states'" (Dewey, 1929/1958, p. 169). Psychology is always primary in this relationship. Communication could not exist without the foundation of mental states. However, mental states can exist quite nicely without the activity of communication (although this is a proposition that will be challenged in later chapters).

What would a communication theory based on these principles look like? David Berlo published one of the first and most influential textbooks in communication in 1960. In it, Berlo (1960) advocated the thesis that:

Meanings are not in messages, that meaning is not something which is discoverable, that words do not really mean anything at all, that dictionaries do not and cannot provide us with meanings. It will be argued that *meanings are in people*, that meanings are covert responses, contained within the human organism. Meanings are learned. They are personal, our own property. We learn meanings, we add to them, we distort them, forget them, change them. We cannot *find* them. They are in *us*, not in messages. Fortunately, we usually find other people who have meanings that are similar to ours. To the extent that people have similar meanings, they can communicate. If they have no similarities between them, they cannot communicate. (p. 175, emphasis in original)

Several important implications follow from Berlo's propositions:

1. Meanings are in people. They are the internal responses that people make to stimuli, and the internal stimulations that these responses elicit.

2. Meanings result from (a) factors in the individual, as related to (b) factors in the physical world around him.

3. People can have similar meanings only to the extent that they have had similar experiences, or can anticipate similar experiences.

4. Meanings are never fixed. As experience changes, meanings change.

5. No two people can ever have *exactly* the same meaning for anything. Many times two people do not even have similar meanings.

6. People will always respond to a stimulus in light of their own meanings.

7. To give people a meaning, or to change their meanings for a stimulus, you must pair the stimulus with other stimuli for which they already have meanings.

(Berlo, 1960, p. 184)

Implications such as these occur frequently in my students' accounts of communication. They are very quick to argue that meanings are created in their minds, or in the minds of their listeners. They explain to me that misunderstandings occur because an idea you may have *within* your mind is not the same as the one *within* my mind. These are just updated versions of Locke's thesis that communication is the transmission of ideas from one mind to another with the dressing of scientific legitimacy conferred by the discourse of the unconscious and the modern cognitive psychology.

In this view, in order to communicate successfully, one must present a message in terms that the receiver already has meanings for. It is no use explaining to your grandmother that her computer is not working because there is an error in her "internal cache." Your grandmother simply does not have the meaning for this language *within* her. This situation also presents me with a potentially significant problem as the author of this book. I know in advance that this book has the potential to be read by hundreds of readers, maybe more. Every reader is unique, and will bring unique meanings and experiences to their reading of this text. There is no way I can write this book so that it corresponds with the unique meanings any individual reader may have. For some readers, this book may be a joy, and will correspond with many meanings and experiences they have had before. For other readers, this book will be difficult and exasperating, if not incomprehensible. Even the same reader can experience both responses. My wife, who has reviewed many drafts of this text, finds some of the chapters clear and informative. Other chapters she finds dense and unclear. Unfortunately, there is no way I can write this book in advance to take into account all of these readers. If I could, my name would be Stephen King!

The dominance of views such as Berlo's serves to place communication studies in a secondary and subservient position with respect to cognitive psychology in the explanation of human communication. It advocates the idea that an understanding of the principles of psychological functioning is primary to an adequate understanding of the human ability to communicate. The act of human communication, conceived in terms such as "encoding," "decoding," "intention," "interpretation," and "transmission," is conceptualized as a *result* of the ability to think, act, and process information. Communication becomes reduced to and dependent upon psychological processes, the domain of another discipline, such that "an understanding of the individual's knowledge, cognitive capacities and emotion is the necessary point of departure for building adequate theories of communication" (Hewes & Planalp, 1987, p. 172).

All of this brings us back to Freud's "true psychical reality" and Hartmann's "golden treasure." Our modern understanding of communication is fundamentally bound up with the belief, passed down to us from the late nineteenth century, that the reality of communication lies somewhere beyond communication-in the unconscious realm of information processing mechanisms that are themselves objective, universal, and capable of scientific description. My students consistently employ this psychological discourse in their descriptions of communication. However, they do not consider themselves to be giving psychological descriptions. Communication, for them, still retains something that is distinct and different from a purely psychological explanation. One reason for this is that the students employ words such as "encode," "decode," "transmit," "sender," and "receiver." These terms do not derive from psychology per se. They are part of a discourse of information theory that arose at the same time as the information processing approach to cognitive psychology in the 1940s and 1950s. As we shall see, these two realms are closely entwined. But information theory was to provide the foundation that would set communication apart as a legitimate subject for social scientific study, and provide the vocabulary that my students employ to this day as part of their common sense understanding of communication. The language of information theory, and its impact on the modern regime of communication, is the subject of the following chapter.

Four
Information and the Mathematical Theory of Communication:
A Very Proper and Discreet Girl

An engineering communication theory is just like a very proper and discreet girl accepting your telegrams. She pays no attention to the meaning, whether it be sad, or joyous, or embarrassing. But she must be prepared to deal with all that comes to her desk. (Warren Weaver)

Up to this point, I have argued that contemporary discourses of communication of the kind articulated by my students are framed by the empirical philosophy of John Locke, the legitimacy derived from an invocation of the unconscious, and the computer metaphor of an information processing paradigm dominant within the field of cognitive psychology. None of these discourses address communication directly. Locke was much more concerned with what happened *within* the mind as opposed to what happened *between* people. Similarly, the discourses of the golden treasure of the unconscious and the development of the information-processing metaphor in psychology were concerned with the problem of how to address the investigation of the human mind in a scientifically legitimate way. At no point was a consideration of communication central to those concerns. As we have seen, cognitive psychology considered communication phenomena as variables that could be manipulated to observe and measure their impact on the underlying information processing system. Information processing research looked beyond words and symbols in order to describe the objective mechanisms that made their production and understanding possible. At no point was it concerned to look outwards, to the use of words in conversation and everyday interaction, a realm riddled with problems of error and lack of experimental control. So how did these particular discourses come to dominate the manner in which my students articulate their understanding of communication? How are they able to assimilate the discursive strands of Locke, the unconscious, and information processing to produce the explanations that are so common in our contemporary regime of communication?

An important place to begin to understand this coalescence is a short book published in 1949 entitled *The Mathematical Theory of Communication* (Shannon & Weaver, 1949). The book consisted of two parts. The main subject of the book was a mathematical treatment of information theory written by Claude Shannon (1949), a mathematician and engineer at Bell Telephone Laboratories. Shannon's thesis was accompanied by a short twenty-eight page introduction, the "Introductory Note on the General Setting of the Analytical Communication Studies," prepared by Warren Weaver (1949), a director of the Rockefeller Foundation from 1932 to 1959. Weaver's introduction suggested ways in which a human communication theory could be developed from Shannon's theorems. In this chapter, the main tenets of Shannon's mathematical theory of communication are described followed by a discussion of Weaver's introduction of Shannon's theory. Of particular importance will be the role Weaver played in bringing communication into the discursive realm of the psychological.

Shannon's Mathematical Theory of Communication

Shannon's theory of communication applied only to one specific aspect of communication: "that of reproducing at one point either exactly or approximately a message selected at another point" (Shannon, 1949, p. 31). Shannon is explicitly concerned with the transmission aspect of communication. He was not concerned with the ambiguous, subjective, and error-prone domain of meaning. Shannon states that:

Frequently the messages have a *meaning*; that is they refer to or
are correlated according to some system with certain physical or
conceptual entities. These semantic aspects of communication
are irrelevant to the engineering problem. (Shannon, 1949, p. 31)

Shannon wants to describe in mathematical terms the process by which a
message, any message, regardless of what it says or what it means, is able
to travel from a source to a destination.

The mathematics by which Shannon attempts to describe this
movement of information are quite formidable to the nonspecialist reader.
However, the five stage model of the communication system which Shannon
presents is very familiar:

1. An *information source* which produces a message or
    sequence of messages to be communicated to the receiving
    terminal;

2. A *transmitter* which operates on the message in some way
    to produce a signal suitable for transmission over the
    channel;

3. The *channel* is merely the medium used to transmit the
    signal from transmitter to receiver;

4. The *receiver* ordinarily performs the inverse operation of
    that done by the transmitter, reconstructing the message
    from the signal; and

5. The *destination* is the person (or thing) for whom the
    message is intended.

(Shannon, 1949, pp. 33-34)

The communication system is able to move signals and messages from
place to place, but it has no interest in or understanding of those messages.
Warren Weaver (1949), in his interpretation of Shannon, suggests that:

An engineering communication theory is just like a very proper
and discreet girl accepting your telegram. She pays no attention
to the meaning, whether it be sad, or joyous, or embarrassing.

But she must be prepared to deal with all that comes to her desk. (p. 27)

The philosopher John Searle's thought experiment of the Chinese Room offers another way to understand the nature of communication as envisaged by Shannon. Searle (1984) asks us to imagine a computer programmer who has written a program that will enable a machine to simulate the understanding of the Chinese language. If the computer is given a question in Chinese, it will match the question against its memory and produce appropriate answers to questions in Chinese. Now suppose that the computer's answers are indistinguishable from those of a native Chinese speaker. Can we say that the computer understands Chinese in the same way that a Chinese speaker understands it? Searle extends the example to make the point that it does not.

Imagine that you are locked in a room and in this room are several baskets full of Chinese symbols. You do not understand a word of Chinese. However, you have been given a rule book in English for manipulating those Chinese symbols. The rules specify the manipulations in terms of their syntax, not their semantics. So a rule might say: "Take a squiggle sign out of basket number one and put it next to a squoggle sign from basket number two." Suppose that some other Chinese symbols are passed into the room, and you are given further rules for passing back Chinese symbols out of the room. Unknown to you, the symbols passed in are called "questions" by the people outside of the room and the symbols you pass back out of the room are called "answers to the questions." Suppose that you become so good at manipulating the symbols that very soon your "answers" are indistinguishable from those of a native Chinese speaker. Even if the people outside the room cannot tell the difference, this doesn't change the fact that *you* are locked in your room shuffling Chinese symbols according to a rule book written in English. Searle (1984) concludes that "on the basis of the situation as I have described it, there is no way you could learn any Chinese simply by manipulating these formal symbols" (p. 32).

In this thought experiment, Searle has described a communication system that allows symbols to pass from a source to a destination. It also has rules for combining and manipulating those symbols in certain ways. But the system itself has no understanding of the symbols it manipulates, or the messages those symbols convey. The communication system has grammar, but no semantics. It is the grammar of the communication system that Shannon describes in his theory. As Umberto Eco (1989) describes, Shannon's mathematical theory of communication sets out to measure information "without any reference to the knowledge of a possible receiver"

(p. 45), which was the central concern of psychologically inspired theories of communication such as Berlo's (1960).

Terms such as "source," "transmitter," and "receiver" occur very frequently in the accounts of communication offered by my students, and the model Shannon describes seems intuitively familiar. In some superficial respects, Shannon's communication system can be seen to resemble Locke's model of communication. However, Shannon does not consider and is not concerned with the psychologies of the sender or the receiver in his articulation of the communication problem. He is not concerned with where this information comes from, or even the content that it conveys. I always go to great lengths to remind my students that Shannon's model is not describing some real-world process. Shannon's theory was a mathematical theory and, to develop this theory, "it is first necessary to represent the various elements involved as mathematical entities, suitably idealized from their physical counterparts" (Shannon, 1949, p. 34).

Information theory represents the link between a scientific theory of communication and an information processing view of the individual. Psychology invokes the information routines of the unconscious as a realm that can be studied apart from the muddy and ambiguous realm of consciousness. Similarly, Shannon's information theory allows us to talk about communication in terms divorced from the muddy and ambiguous realm of meaning, interpretation, and understanding. The concept of information will play a key role in allowing communication to be considered scientifically. In the following section, we turn to a consideration of information.

The Nature of Information

From a physical science perspective, information is an interesting phenomenon because it is so unlike concepts of mass or energy, which both work with a principle of conservation. The sum total of mass and energy always remains constant. But if I have a piece of information, and give it to you, you now have it, but so do I. Not only do I still have it, I may even have it in an improved form as a result of my telling you. It would seem that information is more like a biological entity than a physical one in the sense that it has a generative power to reproduce itself. How can there be a physical theory for something like this?

The first point to be made about Shannon's mathematical theory of communication is that it does not deal directly with information itself, but rather with *physical representations* of the information. Shannon's theory

65

is not concerned with knowledge until it is expressed, written down, or represented in some other way. Information can be represented in many different ways: words, numbers, dots and dashes, electric current in a wire, smoke signals, drum beats, nerve impulses, and so on. Any of these methods for representing information are discrete in character; that is, they all make use of certain minimum indivisible descriptive units. In written speech, there are the letters of the alphabet. You add to a written representation one unit at a time. One can think of adding to a representation of information by a unit amount: a letter, a drum beat, a signal, etc. At the point in which information can be conceived in terms of units and counting, then a mathematical theory of information becomes possible.

At the basic level of indivisible units, there is not much to say beyond "a unit of description has been added" or "not added." Or, in more universal terms, "yes" (a unit has been added) or "no" (a unit has not been added). When we are faced with a "yes-or-no" situation, the mathematician is able to invoke a binary number system. Instead of the familiar decimal system, with its ten digits, a binary system uses only two digits, zero and one. Zero can mean "no" (no unit added) while one can mean "yes" (unit added). This is the number system used by computers.

To understand the relationship between information and binary number systems, think of the game Twenty Questions. The questioner starts out with a store of unknown items of information. The contestant asks a question, and receives the answer "yes" or "no." By asking a series of questions, the questioner closes down, step by step, onto the specific item of information they are after. Questions such as "Is it alive?" or "Is it a plant?" or "Can it be found in my backyard?" can be represented by a sequence of binary digits, such as 0, 1, 1, 0, 1, 0, 1, etc. where the first question was answered "no" (0), the second question "yes" (1), the third question "yes" (1), and so on. The information is represented by a series of binary digits.

According to Shannon, the information value of a particular selection is related to the probability of it being selected. In the Twenty Questions game, the *information* associated with a message is measured by the number of questions you have to ask in order to close down on that particular message. The more binary choices necessary, the more unexpected is the item that is revealed, and the more information is present in the process. For Shannon, then, a message with a high probability of selection carries relatively less information. It takes less "yes" or "no" questions to arrive at the answer.

Information is an additive quantity, something that is added to what one already knows. The information contained in any particular message is always relative to the expectations and prior knowledge of the receiver. A remark has high information content if it is unexpected. For example, I live in Morristown, New Jersey. In the summertime, it gets very hot. If, on August 16, I listen to the weather forecast and I hear "Tomorrow, no snow," the amount of information I receive is very limited. I could have reached the same conclusion based on my own experience and the fact that today's temperature was 95 degrees. The probability of there being no snow on August 17 is extremely high, and so telling me this on the weather forecast carries virtually no information value for me. On the other hand, if the forecaster says "Tomorrow, snow," then the amount of information I get is quite considerable, given the improbability of such an event. It is on this general principle that Shannon is able to measure the information value of any particular message being transmitted through a communication channel. It is not *what is said* that is important, but rather the *probability of what is said* being selected from all the things that could be said. Weaver (1967) describes the principle this way:

> In the mathematical theory the word information does not at all refer to the *meaning* of the particular message selected. Indeed, it refers hardly at all to the particular message selected, but rather to the potentialities of message selection from this particular source. How many messages does this source offer, and how probable or improbable of selection are they-and, accordingly, how *unexpected* is a message thus selected? (p. 208)

The message source from which particular messages are selected can be thought of as being like a huge filing cabinet which contains very many but still a finite number of messages. This filing cabinet is constructed so that it is easier to get at some messages than others. This design means that if you are about to select a message from this cabinet, you are more likely to select certain messages and less likely to select others. For example, words such as "a," "of," or "the" give less information since they occur more frequently than words such as "sad," "ounce," or "escape." Each individual message is associated with a probability; the probability that it will be the next to be selected.

The filing cabinet is constructed in such a way that the ease of accessing the various messages is influenced by the preceding choice, and perhaps several preceding choices. This design means that the probability for selection of various messages is dependent on what the past selection of messages has been. My students often tell me that their ability to communicate means that they are free to choose any message they wish. Being raised in the American culture, this belief in any individual having freedom of speech is not surprising. My students tell me that, as free individuals, they can conceive an original idea of their choosing and then encode that idea so they can then express that idea to someone else. But, as Shannon points out, one cannot go to the filing cabinet and just select *any* messages. The cabinet is structured to make certain messages more probable than others. For example, suppose we are dealing with a message source that has words, rather than whole messages, filed in it. We produce a message by successively choosing one word after another. Suppose I have selected the words:

"I would like to _____."

I am now ready to select the next word. Am I totally free to make any choice? The answer is no. The probabilities are exceedingly low, if not zero, that the next word would be "gorilla" or "brown." It is much more probable to be a verb form, such as "go" or "watch TV" or "read."

The same is true of the rigorous structures imposed by certain forms of poetry, with techniques such as rhyme, rhythm, and meter. In a rhyming poem, a distinct vowel sound is deliberately repeated at a specific distance from the place where it was last heard. Since it is known that at a certain place in the text a certain vowel sound will be found (and not any sound), the chances of predicting what the word will be are greatly increased. Given the incomplete phrase:

"Jack and Jill went up the _____,"

we can determine with some accuracy that the missing word might be "hill." The redundancy imposed by the rhyme makes the message easier to remember because of the clues in the text that point to what comes next. Thus we are able to remember, word for word, songs, nursery rhymes, folk-songs, ballads, and, worse luck, advertising jingles.

Given that you have combined a number of words to form a sentence, the message source also constrains the sentences you can utter and still have that sentence make sense. The sentence must make sense relative to the co-text which surrounds it and what this co-text is about. Consider this dialogue adapted from Deetz and Stevenson (1986, p. 75):

CARL: "Dan put a penny in the parking meter today without being picked up."
SHERI: "Did you take him to the record store?"
CARL: "No, the shoe repair shop."

SHERI: "What for?"
CARL: "I got some new shoelaces for my shoes."
SHERI: "Your loafers need heels badly"

At each point in this dialogue, each utterance is both an evocative and responsive act. Each utterance is evocative because it evokes a response from the other person. So when Carl says that his four-year-old son Dan put a penny in the parking meter without having to be lifted up by him, Sheri asks:

"Did you take him to record store?"

There are any number of things Sheri could have said in response, such as:

"Why did you stop?"
"Was Dan excited?" or
"That's great!"

However, there are many more utterances that Sheri would not say, such as:

"John Locke was the first to articulate a transmission view of communication." or
"Claude Shannon is my hero."

Such utterances are simply inappropriate responses to Carl's statement. At the same time, Sheri's response to Carl is also an evocative act, in that it will evoke a response from Carl. Sure enough, Carl replies:

"No, the shoe repair shop."

Again, Carl's response is limited by the nature of Sheri's utterance that preceded it. The pattern of evocation/response/evocation continues to form a unit called "the conversation." Within the pattern of the conversation, both participants are obliged to make appropriate as opposed to random utterances. What is deemed "appropriate" is determined by the co-text of the surrounding utterances. Each utterance has a place in the sequence of this conversation. It is both a response to the utterance that came before it and the impetus for the utterance that follows it. Not only is the content of the utterance derived from the context of the other utterances, but the content of the surrounding utterances are themselves derived from the presence of this utterance in a reflexive relationship. Within the context of a conversation, an individual is never totally free to select *any* utterance or message. She is always constrained by the probabilities imposed by the preceding words, sentences, and utterances.

The probability of any particular message being selected from the message source is also determined by the nature of sentence structure. So deeply ingrained is our knowledge of sentence structure, we have no difficulty in recognizing nonsense sentences such as:

"The mentitious nargots pounted cropfully."

Although the sentence conveys nothing semantically relevant, it does communicate its own sentence structure. One can recognize the parts of the sentence: adjective, noun, verb, and adverb. Given the construction alone, it is possible to deduce that this is a statement rather than a question.

The occurrence of a word can also be predicted by its place within a particular sentence. For example:

"In the United States, the Fourth of July is a _____."
"The _____ of snow is white."
"The auditorium in our _____ has poor _____."
"He is a _____ carrier."

All of these examples represent the workings of a *syntactic system*; a set of rules for combining words. We might refer to these as the rules of a grammar such as subject-verb-object constructions within English. The syntactical structures of a message ensure that, to some extent, an addressee will already know what will be said in a given situation, or at a given place in a text. They provide a structure to communicative acts that limit the range of possible interpretations an addressee can give to a message. This structure is the heart of Shannon's mathematical theory of communication. It shows that the response of an addressee can take place independently of the content of the words. A reader does not need to have any notion of what "mentitious nargot" refers to in order to derive some understanding of the expression "The mentitious nargots pounted cropfully." She can do so purely on the basis of the syntactic system and the system of probabilities which govern their combination.

When I select out of a message source, I have a certain amount of freedom of selection. I would have a larger freedom of selection if there were no probability hangover from selections made in the past. Divide the actual freedom of action (constrained by past selections) by the larger, maximum freedom of action if I were totally unconstrained by past selections. Suppose this division produces the ratio 8/10. This ratio means that (a) I am 8/10ths as free to choose as I would be if uninfluenced by past selections, or (b) that 2/10ths of my maximum possible freedom of selection is removed because of the statistical linkages that exist between messages, or words, or symbols, in the source.

This 2/10 of lost freedom is called redundancy. When we talk, we have this idea that we are free to choose words, one at a time. This is an illusion. Unless we talk complete and jumbled nonsense, where each word is totally unrelated to the words before it, I have to form sentences within the normal statistical framework of English speech. English speech is approximately 50 per cent redundant. About half the choice is up to you, the other half automatically results from the common basis of agreement concerning the way English is put together.

Apart from the five-part schematic of Shannon's communication system, it seems clear that there is very little in common between Shannon's mathematical theory of communication and the descriptions of communication given by my students. My students simply do not talk in terms of the probabilities of messages being selected from a source. They see messages in terms of meaning and content, rather than signals where meaning is "irrelevant to the engineering problem" (Shannon, 1949, p. 31). How can one explain the profound impact that Shannon's model had on contemporary ways of speaking about communication when it had little, if any, direct application to human communication at all. Everett Rogers (1986) claims that the publication of this book was "the most important single turning point in the history of communication science" (p. 85) while Rogers and Valente (1993) suggest that "Shannon's information theory provided the root paradigm for the field of communication theory and research" (p. 50). Clearly it is not Shannon's mathematical theory of communication alone that has secured its place in our contemporary discursive regime of communication. There is something else that contributed to its influence. We can find that something else in Weaver's (1949) "Introductory Note on the General Setting of the Analytical Communication Studies." Here we can find Shannon's mathematical theory of communication contextualized within a Lockean view of the mind, the discourse of the unconscious, and the information processing paradigm of cognitive psychology. Combine these elements and you find the contours of the discourse of communication articulated by my students.

71

Not Particularly Concerning Shannon

The word communication *will be used here in a very broad sense to include all procedures by which one mind may affect another. (Warren Weaver)*

It is in Weaver's (1949) "Introductory Note on the General Setting of the Analytical Communication Studies," rather than Shannon's treatise itself, that we find the immersion of a mathematical theory of communication into a Lockean discourse of minds. Weaver's involvement with Shannon's work is recounted by Weaver (1967) as an anecdote:

> I became involved with this . . . subject through a conversation in the lunchroom of the Rockefeller Foundation. That organization's president, from 1948 to 1952, was the gifted Chester I. Barnard, known in the industrial world as the former chief executive of the Bell Telephone Company of New Jersey, to the world of scholarship for his knowledge of sociology and language, and to his friends for his beautiful playing of the piano. Chester asked me one day at lunch if I had seen a recent paper by Claude Shannon, in the *Bell System Technical Journal*, on a mathematical theory of communication. Yes, I had read the article. Did I understand it? Yes, I did. Could the results be stated in more generally understandable terms?
>
> Having always believed the dictum-was it not Faraday who said this-that *any* scientific result can be made understandable if the scientific expositor only uses enough skill, patience, and care, I recklessly answered Chester Barnard in the affirmative. And he promptly told me (and he was, after all, my boss) to go ahead and write out an understandable statement of the Shannon theory. (p. 197-198)

The foundation of Weaver's interpretation of Shannon was to situate Shannon's subject matter with respect to a broader range of communication questions. Thus Weaver identified three levels of communication problems:

Level A - How accurately can the symbols of communication be transmitted?

Level B - How precisely do the transmitted symbols convey the desired meaning?

Level C - How effectively does the received meaning affect conduct in the desired way?

The purpose of proposing the three category system is to situate Shannon's theory as a response to the Level A problem of communication, the issue of accuracy in transmission, and to clearly differentiate it from Levels B and C. Weaver went to great lengths to point out that Shannon's theory was not concerned with the semantic or effectiveness dimensions. Weaver (1949) stressed that "*information* must not be confused with meaning" (p. 8); that "this word information in communication theory relates not so much to what you *do* say, as to what you *could* say" (p. 8); and also that information theory is concerned with the statistical nature of the information source and "is not concerned with the individual messages (and not at all directly concerned with the meaning of the individual messages) (p. 14). It is clearly explained that this approach to information leads to a set of research questions that does not relate directly to human communication at all. Weaver (1949) lists them as follows:

a. How does one measure the *amount of information*?
b. How does one measure the *capacity* of a communication channel?
c. The action of the transmitter in changing the message into the signal often involves a *coding process*. What are the characteristics of an efficient coding process? And when the coding is as efficient as possible, at what rate can the channel convey information? (p. 8)

Weaver introduced levels B and C in order to demonstrate that Shannon's theory was NOT concerned with problems such as these. Yet it is precisely the issues raised by these levels that have entered into the contemporary regime of communication. When reading Weaver's introduction, it becomes clear that Weaver could not resist the temptation to speculate on questions that go beyond the territory laid out by Shannon. Weaver admits as much as he recounts how he came to write his introduction:

The final result, however, was a reasonably clear explanation which made little use of mathematical terms, and which also explored some aspects of the theory which had not particularly concerned Shannon. (Weaver, 1967, p. 198)

Of particular interest here is Weaver's treatment of those "aspects of the theory which had not particularly concerned Shannon" since it was these, rather than Shannon's original theory, that were to drive much of the interest in Shannon's model. Rogers (1986) writes that much of the impact Weaver was to have on the field was "unfortunate" (p. 86) since Shannon's mathematical theory of communication was clearly inappropriate for understanding the subtlety of human interaction. Yet this did not prevent Weaver from speculating on levels B and C, which explicitly address issues of meaning and the relationship of meaning with human behavior, in terms far different than Shannon's engineering orientation. This emphasis is clear in the opening sentence of Weaver's introduction, which reads as follows:

> The word *communication* will be used here in a very broad sense
> to include all procedures by which one mind may affect another.
> (Weaver, 1949, p. 3)

In the very first sentence, the reference to Locke's discourse of communication is apparent. Locke spoke of the end of communication as being the excitation of an idea in the mind of a listener created by the speech produced by the mind of a speaker. Weaver expounds this discourse by taking the categories of Shannon's model of an idealized communication system, to be treated as idealized mathematical entitles, and treating them as if they were mental operations of minds and brains. For example, Weaver (1949) writes:

> In oral speech, the information source is the brain, the transmitter
> is the voice mechanism producing the varying air pressure (the
> signal) which is transmitted through the air (the channel). (p. 7)

Further, Weaver (1949) states that:

> The *receiver* is a sort of inverse transmitter, changing the
> transmitted signal back into a message, and handing this message
> on to the destination. When I talk to you, my brain is the
> information source, yours the destination; my vocal system is the
> transmitter, and your ear and the associated eighth nerve is the
> receiver. (p. 7)

This is the kind of talk my students routinely give me when I ask them about communication. They will even use terms such as "information source," "encoding," and "decoding."

Weaver moves significantly beyond Shannon, and into the contemporary discursive regime of communication that my students are all so familiar with, in his speculations on the application of the mathematical theory of communication to understanding how messages are interpreted and understood. Thus Weaver (1949) explicitly discusses communication problems encountered at level B, those concerned with meaning:

> The *semantic problems* are concerned with the identity, or satisfactorily close approximation, in the interpretation of meaning by the receiver as compared with the intended meaning of the sender. This is a very deep and involved situation. (p. 4)

How receivers are able to interpret symbols is not a mathematical or engineering question. It is a psychological question. It asks by what means is the human mind able to extract meaning from symbols. The only answer Weaver has to give is that it is a "very deep and involved situation." In another article, Weaver refers to this activity of extracting meaning as taking place "through some as yet unknown mind-brain process" (Weaver, 1967, p. 205). Weaver is taking Shannon's mathematical model of communication into the discourse of psychology, unknown mental processes, the unconscious, and the problem of discovering those information processing routines in the brain which enable interpretation to occur. Weaver is bringing communication back to familiar ground, the difference being that Shannon's theory is not a philosophy, but a rigorous mathematical system.

Wilbur Schramm was instrumental in taking Weaver's reading of Shannon's theory and making it the foundation of the fledgling field of communication research (see Rogers & Valente, 1993). Schramm's conceptualization of communication was essentially drawn along the level A flow chart provided by Shannon and the levels B and C speculations provided by Weaver. For example, Schramm (1954) writes:

> A *source* may be an individual (speaking, writing, drawing, gesturing) or a communication organization (like a newspaper, publishing house, television station, or motion picture studio). The *message* may be in the form of ink on paper, sound waves in the air, impulses in electric current, a wave of the hand, a flag in the air, or any other signal capable of being interpreted meaningfully. The *destination* may be an *individual* listening, watching, or reading; a member of a *group,* such as a discussion group, a lecture audience, a football crowd, or a mob; or an individual member of a particular group we call the mass

audience, such as the reader of a newspaper or a viewer of television. (pp. 3-4)

Using Shannon's model, almost any act of communication could be broken down into a source, a message, and a receiver. Weaver (1949) states that Shannon's theory of communication can apply "not only written and oral speech, but also music, the pictorial arts, the theatre, the ballet, and in fact all human behavior" (p. 3). Indeed, Weaver does not limit communication to uniquely human activity. He advocates that:

It may be desirable to use a still broader definition of communication, namely, one which would include the procedures by means of which one mechanism (say automatic equipment to track an airplane and to compute its probable future positions) affects another mechanism (say a guided missile chasing this airplane). (Weaver, 1949, p. 3)

It really does not matter what particular communication situation or medium is being referred to because, according to Weaver, the underlying communication competence is always the same. Weaver considered Shannon's theory to be addressing a process as fundamental and universal as Einstein's statement that $E=MC^2$. Weaver (1949) writes:

This is a theory so general that one does not need to say what kinds of symbols are being considered-whether written letters or words, or musical notes, or spoken words, or symphonic music, or pictures. The theory is deep enough so that the relationships it reveals indiscriminately apply to all these and to other forms of communication. (p. 25)

and that:

This means, of course, that the theory is sufficiently imaginatively motivated so that it is dealing with the real inner core of the communication problem-with those basic relationships which hold in general, no matter what special form the actual case may take. (p. 25)

Weaver takes from Shannon a "real inner core" of communication; a reality that lies beyond all appearances, no matter what form those appearances take. The inner core is like the inner realm of the unconscious.

It lies beyond what we can see and experience and moves the reality of communication to some other place. The study of communication is no longer associated with any particular meaning or behavior. It is now a general principle which can be used to explain any and all meaning and behavior in terms of Shannon's universal theorems.

Communication, Effectiveness, and Control

My students have been brought up in a regime of communication where Shannon's model of communication and Weaver's speculations on it have become part of the real world they live in. The "sender-message-receiver" equation is, for them, the real inner core of what it means to communicate. It is not their place to question this. Instead, their main concern is how to exploit it. How can we use this knowledge of communication to achieve specific communication ends, such as giving an effective speech or writing an effective report?

My students are very concerned with effectiveness in their accounts of communication. For many, communication is not a philosophical question to be reflected upon, but a tool with which to do things. Their discussion is most often framed in the context of the communication professions such as journalism, public relations, advertising, and corporate communication. Some of my students work in these industries already. When I probe further and ask "What is the nature of communication within these industries?" their answers are readily forthcoming. Communication is a tool to achieve desired attitudes and behaviors in the receiver. The end may be to persuade someone to buy a product, to remain loyal to a corporate brand, or interpret a world event in a particular way. My students want to know how to use communication strategically to bring about desired outcomes in particular audiences or targets. In short, my students want to be able to persuade and influence others.

One of the key embellishments Warren Weaver added in his interpretation of Shannon's mathematical theory of communication was the introduction of the level C category of communication problems-the problems of effectiveness:

> The *effectiveness problems* are concerned with the success with which the meaning conveyed to the receiver leads to the desired conduct on his part. It may seem at first glance undesirably narrow to imply that the purpose of all communication is to influence the conduct of the receiver. But with any reasonably

broad definition of conduct, it is clear that communication either affects conduct or is without any discernible and probable effects at all. (p. 5)

In his "Introductory Note," Weaver (1949) justified his inclusion of level C problems of effectiveness by referencing another gifted mathematician, Norbert Wiener. As Weaver (1949) remarks in a footnote to his "Introductory Note," "Dr. Shannon has himself emphasized that communication theory owes a great debt to Professor Norbert Wiener for much of its basic philosophy" (p. 3). Weaver (1949) then adds the following:

Shannon has naturally been specially concerned to push the applications to engineering communication, while Wiener has been more concerned with biological application (central nervous system phenomena, etc.). (p. 3)

Wiener will provide the discursive bridge between Shannon's engineering theory and the scientifically legitimated study of mental processes in terms of information processing. Wiener will use communication as the means by which an information processing system can interact with and respond appropriately to its environment. Like Shannon, Wiener will describe this interaction in rigorous mathematical language. Wiener (1954) called his view of communication by the term "cybernetics," and it remains an integral part of our modern regime of communication.

Cybernetics is a broad term which embraces many different aspects of what Wiener (1954) terms "the theory of messages" (p. 15). These aspects include the electrical engineering theory of the transmission of messages of the kind developed by Shannon. However, Wiener goes on to expand upon "a few ideas shared by Drs. Claude Shannon, Warren Weaver, and myself" (p. 16) into an established field of research, which included:

- the study of language
- the study of messages as a means of controlling machinery and society
- the development of computing machines and other such automata
- certain reflections upon psychology and the nervous system

The central thesis driving Wiener's (1954) study of cybernetics is that "society can only be understood through the study of messages and the communication facilities that belong to it" (p. 16). However, Wiener is using the word "communication" in a particular way that is much more closely related to Weaver's level C problem of communication effectiveness than it is to Shannon's level A problem of transmission accuracy. For Wiener, communication and control are inherently linked. When I communicate with someone, my act of communication is always an attempt to control the response I wish the receiver to make to my message. As Wiener (1954) explains, "when I give an order to a person . . . I am aware of the order that has gone out and of the signal of compliance that has come back" (p. 16). Therefore, communication is "control" in the sense that the behavior of the receiver is a response to the communication behavior of the sender. Conversely, control is also communication, since "when I control the actions of another person, I communicate a message to him" (Wiener, 1954, p. 16). Wiener (1954) continues: "Furthermore, if my control is to be effective I must take cognizance of any messages from him which may indicate that the order is understood and has been obeyed" (p. 16). In other words, the response of the receiver acts as *feedback* which the sender can use to modify future messages until the desired response is obtained.

Within this framework of message-response (feedback)-message, Wiener (1954) sees very little difference between whether or not the communication is taking place between people, or "between man and machines, between machines and man, and between machine and machine" (p. 16). As Wiener remarks:

> To me, personally, the fact that the signal in its intermediate stages has gone through a machine rather than through a person is irrelevant and does not in any case greatly change my relation to the signal. (p. 16)

Like Warren Weaver, Wiener wants to reduce communication to the "real inner core of the communication problem-with those basic relationships which hold in general, no matter what special form the actual case may take" (Weaver, 1949, p. 25). Like Shannon's mathematical theory of communication, Wiener's cybernetic theory of messages will apply to any communication system, whether it is embodied in a biological system, a mechanical system, or a social system. As a result, Wiener's concepts of feedback and self-correction held out the promise of a rich and rigorously formulated frame work for studying human behaviors (Eden, 1983; Elias, 1983; Kochen, 1983).

Wiener also whole-heartedly adopts an information processing metaphor of mental states in his explanation of communication and control in people. Wiener (1954) writes:

> Man is immersed in a world which he perceives through his sense organs. Information that he receives is co-ordinated through his brain and nervous system until, after the proper process of storage, collation, and selection, it emerges through effector organs, generally his muscles. (p. 17)

In Wiener's (1954) model, "information is a name for the content of what is exchanged with the outer world as we adjust to it, and make our adjustment felt upon it" (p. 17).

Wiener's discourse of communication and control, especially his account of the role of mental processing of sensory data in the production of feedback, plays a central role in the accounts of communication given by my students. My students comfortably talk of communication in terms of physical signals being picked up by their senses and then "processed" by their minds. In the case of oral speech, that sense is hearing. The signal enters the ear, is transformed into a signal that runs along a nerve to the brain. When I ask the students what the brain does with this signal, they reply with words such as "process," "access," and "decode." When pushed further, they will eventually resort to a neurophysiological language to express the same ideas: "synaptic firing," "neural networks," and "electro-chemical processes." They are expressing to me their belief that communication must eventually be understood and expressed in terms of physical signals being acted upon by physical processes located in physical nerve pathways in a physical brain.

This mode of explanation is clear in Wiener's description of the actions of a kitten. Wiener (1954) writes: "I call to the kitten and it looks up. I have sent it a message which it has received by its sensory organs, and which it registers in action" (p. 22). This example illustrates Wiener's connection of communication with control. Wiener's call to the kitten and the reception of that call by the kitten's sensory organs causes a response in the kitten's mental processes. As a result of these processes, the kitten acts in a manner consistent with the message to which it has been exposed. The act of communication has controlled some part of the kitten's behavior by structuring the response the kitten produces.

However, Wiener is also interested in another sense of the relationship between communication and control. Information received from the environment will also create messages *within* the kitten's nervous system.

Wiener goes on to describe the kitten batting at a swinging spool. The spool swings to the left and the kitten is able to catch it with his left paw. Wiener (1954) remarks that "this time messages of a very complicated nature are both sent and received within the kitten's own nervous system through certain nerve-end-bodies in its joints, muscles, and tendons" (p. 22). In this case, Wiener is not talking about communication *between* people (or people and machines) but rather communication between different parts of an *internal* communication system, in this case the nervous system of the kitten. This internal communication system is totally beyond the conscious experience or control of the organism. As such it constitutes an entirely autonomous system, beyond the subjective nature of human consciousness, and capable of objective investigation and description. This detachment from consciousness is clear from Wiener's (1954) example of what happens when he picks up his cigar:

> If I pick up a cigar, I do not will to move any specific muscles.
> Indeed in many cases, I do not know what those muscles are.
> What I do is to turn into action a certain feedback mechanism;
> namely a reflex in which the amount by which I have yet failed
> to pick up the cigar is turned into a new and increased order to
> the lagging muscles, whichever they may be. (p. 26)

So, here is the situation. You see a cigar and you want to pick it up. In some sense, you "will" your arm and your hand to do this. However, you do not "will" any specific muscles or nerve to do this. This "willing" is very general. The actual picking up of the cigar is carried out by muscles of which the owner is unaware, in an order and sequence that Wiener cannot conceive or control. The muscles, it seems, retrieve the cigar through a system of reflexes and feedback. They sense and monitor the distance and orientation of the cigar with respect to the body, and then move on the basis of this *feedback*.

Machines such as photo-electric door openers can exhibit the same properties and propensities as Wiener picking up his cigar. Photoelectric doors possess sense organs; photoelectric cells which change electrically when a light falls on them. These machines with receptors, like Wiener or the kitten, are conditioned by their relation with the external world. The object of knowledge to be addressed in this view of communication and control is not the individual, or the meanings of messages received by the individual. The cybernetic account equates communication with the mechanical operations of a physical nervous system and its machine counterparts. In other words, the act of communication and the act of information processing become the *same thing*. Communication is simply the outcome of an internal information processing system, and the process of information is itself a form of communication.

We see in Wiener's discourse many of the contours of my students' regime of communication: Communication is something internal which can be manipulated by outside influences. What the students require of me is that I teach them the appropriate skills and methods by which such influence can be achieved. How do I get an audience to comprehend and act upon my message? To like me? To buy my product? To have a positive image of my company?

My students are not unique in holding this desire to be able to use communication as means to achieve their desired ends. This motivation was the impetus of the development of communication into a distinct discipline in the 1950s, the period immediately following the publication of Shannon and Weaver's mathematical model of communication and Wiener's treatise on cybernetics. My students are always surprised when I tell them that the systematic study of communication is a very recent phenomenon. Many students believe communication studies, *as they know it* within the transmission regime, began in antiquity, perhaps with the Greeks. However, we know from chapter two that the transmission view of communication was not articulated systematically until John Locke's (1690/1975) essay was published in 1690. It wasn't until the 1950s that communication was taken seriously as a subject for social scientific attention and study. Historian Christopher Simpson (1994) notes that communication research crystalized into a distinct discipline, complete with colleges, curricula, and the authority to grant doctorates, between 1950 and 1955.

Simpson (1994) points out that much of the impetus for shaping communication research into a distinct scholarly field was not a detached, scholarly interest in "the nature of communication." Like the accounts offered by my students, these initial motivations were dominated by very pragmatic concerns. My students think of communication as a tool. In the 1950s, the same view was prevalent, the only difference being that communication was considered as a particular type of tool-*a weapon of war*. The systematic study of communication as we know it today within the transmission regime found its initial impetus and nourishment from government sponsored psychological warfare programs where "psychological warfare" was defined as:

> A group of strategies and tactics designed to achieve the ideological, political, or military objectives of the sponsoring organization (typically a government or political movement)

through the exploitation of a target audience's cultural-psychological attributes and its communication system. (Simpson, 1994, p. 11)

Simpson (1994) reports, for example, that during this period, the CIA clandestinely underwrote the Bureau of Social Science Research (BSSR) studies of torture of prisoners of war. The CIA reasoned that interrogation of captives could be understood as "simply another application of the social-psychological principles articulated in communication studies" (p. 4).

Sponsoring groups of United States military, propaganda, and intelligence industries naturally favored a particular applied and pragmatic approach to communication research that would further their miliary and ideological aims. This perspective offered both an explanation of what communication "is" and a box of tools for examining it. In this context, communication was conceptualized and investigated as an instrument for persuading or dominating targeted groups. Communication was understood as little more than a transmission mechanism into which virtually any kind of message could be plugged to achieve ideological, political, or military goals. As Simpson (1994) describes:

U.S. military and intelligence agencies became instrumental in the systematic elaboration of an interlocking series of concepts about communication that have defined much of post-World War II communication research . . . Cold War-era psychological warfare studies provided extensive, selective funding for large scale projects designed to elaborate, test, and publicize the possibilities of communication-as-domination. They helped create networks of sympathetic insiders who enjoyed control over many aspects of scholarly publishing, rank and tenure decisions, and similar levers of power within academe. In doing so, these programs contributed significantly to the triumph of what is today regarded as mainstream communication research over its rivals in U.S. universities. (pp. 8-9)

This view of communication as domination and psychological warfare followed easily from the Lockean-information processing-information theory derived discourse of communication. It formed the basis of many influential statements and theories in the early days of communication research. Perhaps the most famous expression of these was that articulated by Harold Lasswell (1948, p. 37), who suggested that "a convenient way to describe an act of communication is to answer the following questions":

Who
Says What
In Which Channel
To Whom
With What Effects?

This model seems so simple and so commonsense to us today it is difficult to argue that communication could not be this way. As Simpson (1994) notes, Lasswell's dictum is "practically inscribed in stone over the portals of those U.S. colleges offering communication as a field of study" (p. 19). The influence of Lasswell's dictum can be seen in the early textbooks of communication studies, such as *The Process of Communication* by David Berlo (1960) where Berlo writes:

> *We communicate to influence - to affect with intent.* In analyzing communication, in trying to improve our own communication ability, the first question we need to ask is, what did the communicator intend to have happen as a result of his message? What was he trying to accomplish, in terms of influencing his environment? As a result of his communication, what did he want people to believe, to be able to do, to say? In psychological terms, what response was he trying to obtain? (p. 12, emphasis in original)

Berlo (1960) adds:

> All communication behavior has as its purpose, its goal, the production of a response. When we learn to phrase our purposes in terms of specific responses from those attending to our messages, we have taken the first step toward efficient and effective communication. (p. 12)

The confluence of these various interests and ways of speaking about communication, ranging from the philosophy of John Locke, the discourse of the unconscious, the mind as a processor of information, Shannon's mathematical description of the communication channel, Wiener's systematic connection of communication with control, and the United States Government's funding of social scientists to conduct studies of psychological warfare, came to produce a regime of communication that is neatly summarized by James Carey (1977) as follows:

American studies are grounded in a transmission or transportation view of communication. They see communication, therefore, as a process of transmitting messages at a distance for the purpose of control. The archetypal case of communication, then, is persuasion, attitude change, behavior modification, socialization through the transmission of information, influence, or conditioning. (p. 412)

This, it seems to me, is where my students stand today in the accounts they give in response to my question "What is communication?" They are extremely comfortable giving these accounts. They see very little in the way of challenges to such accounts. When I badger them with my questions and push them down linguistic dead ends, my students' faith and belief in a transmission regime as articulated by Carey is almost unshakable. In the chapters that follow, I intend to shake this regime somewhat by introducing ways of speaking about communication that do not rely on a vocabulary that includes such terms as "transmission," "control," or "influence." But I want to approach these alternative discourses slowly. If we go too quickly, the language they speak will appear almost incomprehensible. Before we go there, I need to introduce some nagging seeds of doubt.

For example, like the cognitive psychologists before them, my students are very secure in their belief that communication is always the *product* of underlying mental states. But what if I could demonstrate and persuade you of the opposite? Suppose I could make you believe that mental states were the product of communication? Impossible? Maybe not. If we can make this step together, you will be ready to begin speaking within regimes of discourse that are very different from the regime of communication that currently has such a strong grip on our language, our reality, and our selves. It's time to start rattling that cage.

Five

How Information Processing Became More Like Communication:
Communication, Memory, and Subliminal Perception:

Compared with other organisms, never mind persons, mechanisms are somewhat limited. (John Shotter)

I have argued so far that the discourse of experimental psychology, in combination with the empiricist philosophy of knowledge of John Locke and the information theory of Shannon, Weaver, and Wiener, has provided the bedrock upon which the regime of communication has been built. It all seems to make perfect sense. An idea arises in the mind of the sender. The sender encodes this idea and transmits it to a receiver, who decodes the message and derives from it an idea that is similar to, though not exactly the same as, the idea in the mind of the sender. Psychology is important because it holds out the promise of being able to look beyond the subjectivity inherent in the encoding of ideas into symbols and the decoding of symbols back into ideas. As Wundt suggested, psychology attempts to look beyond the contingencies of individual acts by focusing on the objective principles by which such encoding and decoding can take place by any person in any situation. The marriage of information theory and psychology offers the pathway to understanding communication's "real inner core," to use Weaver's term, in terms of human information processing.

I ended the previous chapter by stating that I would like to introduce some nagging doubts about this picture. The relationship between psychology and communication seems, on the surface, to be so neat and tidy. Mental states produce communication. What could be more clear and commonsense than that? But a closer consideration soon reveals that all is not as neat and tidy as it should be. For example, I demonstrated earlier that John Locke viewed communication as a fundamental problem. The perfect matching of ideas in the mind of a sender with the ideas in the mind of a receiver is an idealization to be strived for, but is never actually achieved. Even if it were achieved, the participants would have no way of knowing that this was the case! The arbitrary relationship between ideas and words also adds uncertainty to the communication process. In this chapter, I explore two examples of how the subjective and ambiguous nature of communication has seeped into the discourse of cognitive psychology and claimed for itself part of its discursive territory. My two examples describe the work of two prominent cognitive psychologists. Dr. Elizabeth Loftus of the University of Washington at Seattle, is best known for her development of a perceptual theory of eyewitness testimony. Dr. Norman Dixon, of University College, London, is an experimental psychologist interested in why the concept of subliminal perception has proved to be such a controversial subject within the field of cognitive psychology. Neither of these psychologists would claim that they were describing communication in terms like those proposed by John Locke. Yet what is interesting about these two bodies of work is that their theories about mental states become more and more dependent on the subjectivity, ambiguity, and arbitrariness that is inherent in a Lockean view of communication. It is not simply the case that a language of mental states is necessary to describe and understand communication. A language of communication is also a significant factor in the manner in which we describe and understand mental states.

The Malleability of Memory

The malleability of human memory represents a phenomenon that is at once perplexing and vexing. It means that our past might not be exactly as we remember it. The very nature of truth and of certainty is shaken. It is more comfortable for us to believe that somewhere in our brain, however well hidden, rests a bedrock of memory that absolutely corresponds with events that have passed. Unfortunately, we are simply not designed that way. (Elizabeth Loftus)

Take a moment away from reading this book and think about something you did yesterday. As you recall and visualize this event, reflect on what you think your mind is doing as it retrieves this memory and presents it to you. What is happening here? Is your mind doing something like playing a videotape? Is it selecting the appropriate tape from some tape library? Is the tape that is played for you something like a "recording" of the event you have recalled? Most people see memory working in a manner something similar to this. They see memory as an internal mechanism that is able to both store and retrieve information much like the hard drive on your computer. Given the technological metaphors which dominate modern cognitive psychology, this comparison should not be considered surprising.

Elizabeth Loftus began her career as a cognitive psychologist with a similar understanding of memory. Her early published work explored and described the nature of memory as an internal mechanism and a stage in the human information processing system. Loftus's first published article (Loftus, Freedman & Loftus, 1970) reported a relatively simple experiment concerned with the retrieval of information from semantic memory. Remember, semantic memory is our memory of concepts such as "cat," "car," or "building" which enables us to recognize and make sense of unique physical objects we encounter in the world. Information processing models of semantic memory suggest that such concepts are organized in semantic hierarchies. For example, the concept of "canary" might be located in a hierarchal network consisting of the categories:

Living Things -- Animals -- Birds -- Yellow Birds -- Canary

Loftus reasoned that if she compared the time it took to retrieve an example from a subordinate category (e.g., "Yellow Birds") and a superordinate category (e.g., "Animals"), it would be possible to infer whether the retrieval process had to search the whole hierarchy before it came to the relevant information. If this was the case, then it would be reasonable to expect that the search time for the subordinate category would be greater than the superordinate category since the number of semantic levels to be searched is larger. However, despite these expectations, Loftus found that the retrieval times were not significantly different for the two types of category and her study concluded that categories in semantic memory can be located directly without having to travel via a network of hierarchal pathways. What is interesting about this study is not its results per se, but rather Loftus's adherence to a model of memory which is internal and machine-like. When we retrieve a memory of a canary or a bird, Loftus is assuming that this process takes time because the retrieval mechanism has to search, in real time, the categories in the semantic hierarchies before it can retrieve the desired item. In the dark place of our mind, a mechanism is at work whereby information really moves from one place to another.

This experiment is representative of a lot of the published work done by Loftus early in her career. Specific studies investigated topics such as the following:

- The organization of language categories in semantic memory (Loftus, 1972);
- The effect of category names on retrieval time (Loftus & Freedman, 1972);
- Frequency of categories and category members (Loftus & Suppes, 1972);
- Semantic memory and mood (Loftus, Wiksten, & Abelson, 1974);
- The effect of instruction on semantic memory (Loftus & Loftus, 1974);
- Category dominance (Loftus, 1973);
- Retrieval from semantic memory by young children (Loftus & Grober, 1973); and
- Retrieving attribute and name information (Loftus & Cole, 1974).

Loftus's adherence to an information processing view of memory is representative of Thomas Kuhn's (1970) notion of normal science, i.e., the solving of problems or puzzles within an already accepted paradigm. Within normal science, we are free to question our results and our methods, but we would never think to question the proposition that our mind works like a computer. That much is taken for granted. Looking back on this early work, Loftus writes:

It was tedious work, no doubt about it. The theoretical model had been set up years earlier by my Ph.D. advisor, and I was just one of several graduate students, each of us plugged into a specific slot, computing our statistical analyses, feeding our results into a common pot. It occurred to me that my particular job was a little like cutting up carrots to put in a soup. To the left and right of me were other students, equally frenzied and meticulous about cutting up their onions, celery, potatoes, chunks of beef, and then tossing them into the same huge pot. And I couldn't help thinking, All I've done is cut up the carrots. (Loftus & Ketchum, 1991, p. 5)

In 1974, Loftus embarked on a program of research that investigated a special case of retrieval from long-term memory, eyewitness testimony. In her article entitled "Reconstruction of Automobile Destruction: An Example of the Interaction Between Language and Memory" (Loftus & Palmer, 1974), Loftus examined the relationship between language and the retrieval from long-term memory of a realistic and complex event. Undergraduate subjects viewed a film of a traffic accident. Immediately after, subjects were given questions to answer about the accident they had witnessed. However, half of the subjects' questions included:

"About how fast were the cars going when they SMASHED into each other?"

while the other half were asked:

"About how fast were the cars going when they HIT each other?"

It was noted that the "Smash" subjects gave a higher estimate of the speed. A week later, subjects had to answer more questions about the accident, but without seeing the film again. The critical question in the second set of questions was:

"Did you see any broken glass?"

In reality, there was no broken glass depicted in the film. However, because broken glass is likely to be present after a high speed crash, it was hypothesized that more of the "Smash" condition subjects would report "yes" to this question. This hypothesis was verified by the results. In their discussion of these findings, Loftus and Palmer (1974) put forward that the subjects were exposed to two kinds of information about the event. The first is information gained from the original perception of the event. The second is external information supplied after the fact, in this case in the form of questions (information contained in language). Although these two types of information are quite separate, over time they became integrated into one single memory of the event. Therefore, subjects in the "smash" condition may "remember" the non-existent broken glass because it is commensurate with their memory of the event rather than its reality. Loftus concluded that questions asked subsequent to an event can cause a reconstruction in one's memory of that event.

This article marked Elizabeth Loftus's departure from the puzzle solving of normal science because it seemed to contradict the idea that memory was simply a storehouse of events where events were recorded and from which those events could be retrieved. For example, Loftus, Altman, and Geballe (1975) considered the effect of questioning upon a witness' later recollections. After viewing an incident on film, subjects were exposed to active questioning ("did you see the broken glass?") or passive questioning ("tell me what you saw"). On further questioning a week later, it was found the perceptions of the subjects in the two conditions were significantly different. Loftus concluded that whoever interrogates a witness first can influence how an event is subsequently reported.

In a review of this work, Loftus (1975) argued that questions asked immediately after witnessing a fast and complex event can have important effects on responses to questions asked at a later time. If these initial questions contain presuppositions on the existence of objects in the event, then it is likely that the subject will report the existence of these objects at a later time, even if the original presupposition was false (i.e., the object did not exist). This research suggests that such questioning immediately after an event can introduce new and potentially incorrect information which is then added to the subject's memorial representation of that event. Such information can cause a reconstruction or alteration of the subjects perceptual memory.

The implications of these and similar findings are discussed in the book *Eyewitness Testimony* (Loftus 1979a). This book is significant in two ways. First of all it represents the pinnacle of Loftus's work on long-term memory, including her normal science period. Loftus has taken this work and extended it beyond its original domain to produce a major and original contribution to psychological research. She has taken the information processing model and used it to throw light on a very different set of issues. Secondly, it represents a major shift in Loftus's thinking about human memory. Loftus displays doubts about the assumptions of the information processing model of human memory and argues that a different conceptualization of the nature of memory is needed to account for her findings and conclusions about eyewitness testimony. As Loftus (1979a) points out in the preface to the book:

> It is a commonly held belief that information, once acquired by the memory system, is unchangeable, and that errors in memory result either from an inability to find stored information . . . or from errors made during the original perception of the event. An alternative position is that stored information is highly malleable and subject to change and distortion by events (such as misleading questions, overheard conversations). (p. xiii)

If the traditional view of memory is correct, i.e., that experiences are stored in memory in their original form, then external information about the event, such as that contained in questions, would coexist alongside the original but would not alter the original memory. Loftus labels this position the *coexistence hypothesis*. However, Loftus's results suggest a different view of memory, the *alteration hypothesis*, which suggests that memories can be irrecoverably altered by exposure to new information after the event. Loftus's review reveals the traditional view to be increasingly untenable in the face of new research evidence and that the new alteration hypothesis offers a much more realistic account.

The conclusions derived from the eyewitness testimony studies led Loftus to an interest in the malleability of memory in general. This new interest represents another distinct phase in her work because it offers a new perspective for thinking about memory. The traditional view of memory is that it is some wondrous storehouse of knowledge and experiences that can be accessed by the operation of a serial stage cognitive mechanism. In studying this system, the psychologist assumes that this process is ordered, logical and hence predictable and that information stored in long-term memory is based on a faithful reflection of reality. This view may be sufficient for testing hypothetical normal science problems in the laboratory, but is this really the case in real life? Loftus's work on eyewitness recall does not suggest this. According to Loftus, memory can be a subjective, malleable, and distorted thing which may alter its construction of the real experience as it is exposed to different kinds of information.

Loftus (1979b) published a review article entitled "The Malleability of Human Memory" which argued this position. In it she presented evidence which seemed to demonstrate that people's recollections of events can be modified by subsequently introduced information. In 1980, Loftus published the book entitled *Memory: Surprising New Insights into How We Remember and Why We Forget*. It is essentially a book on the information-processing conception of memory, but with one important exception. It regards memory as a fallible entity, and argues that a theory of why we forget and distort information is an important component of a realistic understanding of human information processing. As Loftus (1980) points out in her introduction:

> Many people believe that everything we learn is permanently stored in the mind, even though particular details may not be immediately accessible. With hypnosis or other special techniques, these inaccessible details could eventually be recovered. As we shall see, this belief is now being seriously challenged. New studies suggest that our memories are continually being altered, transformed, and distorted. (p. xiii)

We can see in this work a significant step beyond Loftus's normal science activities of the early 1970s. Loftus is no longer working purely within the boundaries of the given paradigm, she is beginning to question some of its fundamental assumptions. This is not normal science because it marks the generation of new perspectives and theory rather than the verification of an existing and unchallenged paradigm.

This new perspective is interesting from another point of view because it says something fundamental about our common sense assumptions concerning human nature. Usually, our working models present a positive reflection of ourselves as human beings. The information processing model, for example, shows people to be fantastically complex processors capable of handling vast amounts of information smoothly and efficiently. However, Loftus's account has some rather disturbing implications:

> The malleability of human memory represents a phenomenon that is at once perplexing and vexing. It means that our past might not be exactly as we remember it. The very nature of truth and of certainty is shaken. It is more comfortable for us to believe that somewhere in our brain, however well hidden, rests a bedrock of memory that absolutely corresponds with events that have passed. Unfortunately, we are simply not designed that way. (Loftus, 1980, p. 290)

Loftus is not only providing a new perspective for research and theory, but also for how we see ourselves as human beings. Loftus and Greene (1980) demonstrated that the memory for a face was affected by the introduction of subsequent misleading information. This contradicted the view that faces were special in their lack of susceptibility to interference. Loftus and Loftus (1980) published an important review article which argued that, contrary to popular belief, the evidence in no way confirms the view that all memories are permanent and thus potentially recoverable. Loftus (1982) discussed those factors which influence memory and the nature of its constructive processes. She argued that new information is assimilated within existing knowledge and beliefs, causing people to remember only what fits their expectations. Loftus (1981) describes a shift in cognitive psychology towards an increased interest in natural cognition (i.e., how real world information is processed and how memory works in actual situations such as eyewitness testimony). This real world nature of memory is a key feature of Loftus's approach to research and theory.

It is interesting to note that as Loftus's work on memory moves toward the messiness of the real world, she also embraces the messy nature of communication as articulated by John Locke (1690/1975). Locke argued that the idea in the mind of a receiver can never match exactly the idea transmitted from the mind of a sender. One might say that Loftus's work is really a detailed examination of this very problem. For example, consider her work on eyewitness testimony. Loftus is looking at the question of why the message received (as revealed by the subject's recollection) can be so different from the message sent (the scene that is witnessed). What are the variables which influence the magnitude of this anomaly and, most importantly, what are the underlying principles which determine how the message received is constructed from the information contained within message sent? To answer questions like these, it is necessary to view the mind in the same way that Locke proposed in 1690. As Glass, Holyoak, and Santa (1979) point out:

> Sharp divisions cannot be drawn between separate processing stages, because the core of cognition is not a passive long term memory, but an active processor that interacts with the environment. According to this view, tracing the flow of information from peripheral to central stages does not do justice to the interactive nature of the system. (p. vi)

It is no longer feasible to see information processing as simply the movement of sensory input through the stages of an internal communication channel. Within this system, there needs to be another more active sense of communication that views communication as something more than a channel. Loftus has recognized that information processing also involves a sense of interaction between various parts of the system. The problem now, then, is not how can models of information processing inform our understanding of communication, but how can models of communication inform our understanding of information processing.

This proposition is very clear in the case of the hypothesis of subliminal perception which is the subject of one of the most bizarre controversies in cognitive psychology. As Norman Dixon (1971) has noted, this hypothesis "is unique in having initiated what is surely one of the longest lasting, most acrimonious, and, in terms of research done and papers published, time-consuming controversies in the history of psychology" (p. 3). What is interesting about the subliminal perception controversy from our point of view is that in terms of the information processing model, subliminal perception is not a phenomenon that should be considered controversial at all. Subliminal perception only becomes controversial when it is considered as a *form of communication*. This is the subject of the following section.

Subliminal Perception: The Nature of a Controversy

There evidently is something about subliminal perception which invites confusion. But why? What is there about this hypothesis that it should invite such misconceptions? And what is there about it which should make it so attractive to some as it is abhorrent to others? (Norman Dixon)

To most people, the following statements would be considered as common sense:

"Since I did not see it, I could not respond to it."
"If I cannot see or hear it, how do I know it is there? If I do not know it is there, how can I respond to it?"

Statements such as these are based upon our subjective experience of everyday perception. We are aware of stimulus objects in our environment and of responding to these objects. But the form of these statements also implies its opposite, namely that without an awareness of a stimulus, there can be no response to it. If we are attending Colin Cherry's (1953) cocktail party and words are whispered by others that we cannot hear, then we simply cannot respond to those words. The model of perception embodied in these statements is quite straightforward: We see things, and then we react to them. Our reaction, then, is not a reaction to the object per se, but rather to the fact we have seen or heard it. This view of perception is demonstrated in the following flow chart (Dixon, 1971, p. 2):

Stimulus – Receptor – Sensory Processes – Physiological – Response
Processes
Underlying
Phenomenal
Representation

This is a quite straightforward model of human information processing. A stimulus from the environment (e.g., light energy) enters the system via a receptor (e.g., the eye). Rudimentary sensory processing sends a neural signal along to optic nerve to the brain where the "physiological processes underlying phenomenal representation" analyze, order, and categorize the raw feed of information streaming from the eyes and render it suitable for conscious representation. Remember, in the information processing model, everything you see or experience is a product of some underlying internal mechanism. Your conscious experience is "made" for you by processes that are themselves preconscious. Your response to the stimulus is made on the basis of your "experience" of the stimulus, not to the stimulus itself.

The hypothesis of subliminal perception offers a slightly different version of this model. It simply says that an organism may respond to a stimulus that does not achieve phenomenal representation (or conscious awareness). A vast literature of research studies working with stimuli too weak or too fast to achieve conscious representation have repeatedly shown that subjects have the capacity to respond to such stimuli (see Dixon, 1971, 1981). For example, imagine yourself as a participant in Lazarus and McCleary's (1951) classic experiment on subception which claimed to demonstrate that the mind could discriminate between stimuli presented so fast that subjects were not aware of them. You have been asked to view a series of nonsense syllables. When certain nonsense syllables appear, you receive a mild electric shock. These shocks occur consistently whenever these syllables appear. You are then fitted to a Galvanic Skin Response (GSR) meter which measures electrical activity in your skin. When you view the syllables associated with the electric shock, your GSR reading goes up because you are expecting to receive another shock, even when that shock is not forthcoming. You have been conditioned to respond to the syllable.

You are now asked to look into a device called a tachistoscope. The tachistoscope looks like a smaller version of a "What the Butler Saw" machine which used to be popular at English seaside resorts. It is also like looking into the periscope of a submarine. The tachistoscope is able to flash words or images at very precise and high speeds. The experiment begins and you see the word "Cat" flash very quickly and then disappear. The experimenter asks you to report what word, if any, you saw. You say "Cat." A second word, "Dog," is flashed, this time much quicker. You report seeing the word "Dog." Words continue to be flashed by the machine. As the speed gets quicker, it becomes more difficult for you to see the words. After a time, you are aware of a flash of light, but you cannot make out the word that is supposedly there. Eventually, the flashes are so fast you're not even sure there was a flash at all. At the point at which the word is flashed so quickly that you cannot see it, the stimulus is said to be subliminal. The word has been objectively placed before your eyes. However, it is presented and taken away so quickly that you cannot report what it was. To use Dixon's language, it was unable to achieve "phenomenal representation."

Once your threshold for awareness has been determined, nonsense syllables are flashed at subliminal speeds. You are totally unaware that they are there. Some of the syllables are the ones to which you have been conditioned to expect an electric shock, while others have not. If the subliminal perception hypothesis is correct, we would predict that even though you are unaware of the syllables being presented, your information processing system still has the capacity to discriminate between the conditioned and unconditioned syllables. In other words, we would expect to you to record a higher GSR response when the conditioned words are presented subliminally and a lower GSR response when the unconditioned syllables are presented. This is what Lazarus and McCleary found. Subjects were indeed responding to the nonsense syllables as indicated by their GSR responses even though they had no conscious awareness of the presence of those syllables. Dixon (1971, p. 2) diagrams these results as follows:

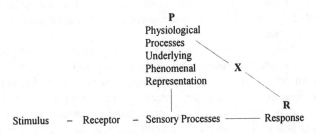

Dixon (1971) defines subliminal perception as the "hypothesis that there are some inputs which may affect R and not P" (p. 3). Dixon also points out that "an obvious, if disturbing, feature of this hypothesis is that there is no logical necessity for the pathway X" (p. 3). It might be argued that since sensory processes affect R directly, it is only those stimuli above a certain energy level that *also* provide phenomenal representation of the stimulus object. In other words, those cerebral processes that give rise to conscious awareness may belong to a system in parallel to the preconscious system of information processing.

Subliminal perception research is the systematic investigation of the relationships between input variables (such as words presented on a tachistoscope) and output variables (such as galvanic skin responses) when the stimulus is denied access to consciousness. The subliminal perception hypothesis asserts that such relationships can be demonstrated with experimental reliability and, to some extent, validity. At this level of discussion, there is nothing particularly controversial about the hypothesis at all. What the hypothesis suggests is that the information processing system is able to process information that is not available to conscious awareness. This is by no means a startling proposition. In fact, all information processing is preconscious until it achieves the status of consciousness. For example, consider memory. When we choose to locate and select certain pieces of information from our long-term memory, we do not consciously recall everything we have ever remembered and consciously search through it. This suggests that there are processes operating preconsciously which can seek out information from long-term memory prior to that selection being raised to the level of conscious experience. A second consideration is the human ability to take in vast amounts of perceptual information from the senses, of which only a small proportion ever achieve conscious awareness. This idea is the familiar concept of "attention," that process by which the human information processing system will attend to that information which is salient to its needs. If we are prepared to accept the concept of attention, then we must also accept that such a process requires a rigorous selection of input at some stage *prior* to its ultimate representation in consciousness. Such a selection would be, by definition, preconscious.

In fact, all sensory stimulation entering the information processing system through the senses can be considered subliminal. It is initially received by the senses outside of consciousness and "made ready" for consciousness by preconscious processes. Experiments on the timing of conscious awareness suggest that consciousness of input does not arise until at least 200 milliseconds after stimuli arrive at the cortical surface (see Libet, 1996). In other words, it takes at least 200 milliseconds of preconscious processing before you can be said to be aware of a stimulus. It also suggests we are constantly 200 milliseconds out of synch with the world we experience. In information processing terms, there is much to do before one can identify a stimulus. Stimuli must be transformed into neural code, analyzed, and compared to concepts in long-term memory before they can be identified. So the idea that sensory input is received and analyzed outside of conscious awareness is not only not controversial, it is an essential part of the information processing model.

The only thing that the subliminal perception hypothesis adds to this account is the proposition that such preconscious processing can lead directly to a response without the necessity of achieving conscious awareness first. Yet, for some reason that Dixon is at a loss to explain, this claim has been the source of great controversy. Dixon (1971) notes that "while a great many psychologists, research workers, and clinicians take it as axiomatic that people may respond to stimuli of which they are unaware, there remains a hardcore of academics, chiefly in the United States, who strenuously deny any such thing" (p. 3). This resistance is puzzling to Dixon because the information processing model of human cognition is explicitly based on a computer metaphor that has no place for a subjective notion of consciousness. As psychologist Geoffrey Underwood (1982) points out:

> We cannot talk about consciousness without talking about experience, but the information processing model of man, one of our strongest conceptual frameworks, does not readily admit the notion of mental experience. Early information processing models of consciousness side-stepped this problem by identifying consciousness with one or more stages of processing-it became a box in the much parodied flowchart. This not only failed to provide an adequate description, but also avoided the question, and provided little in the way of an understanding of how mechanism can incorporate mental experience. (p. viii)

Yet it is those people who adhere most strongly to an information processing perspective who most strenuously oppose the subliminal perception hypothesis. Dixon (1971) writes:

> It is an odd paradox, to say the least, that those *most* concerned to view the human organism as a machine without a psyche, should be the ones *most* resistant to the idea that the object of their study might be able to receive and process information without such an unmachine-like aid as consciousness (p. 5).

In the quote above before Dixon's, I cite Dr. Geoffrey Underwood who is an experimental psychologist at the University of Nottingham in England.

Dr. Underwood has a special place in my academic biography since I interviewed with him to take a Ph.D. under his direction at Nottingham. My subject was to be subliminal perception. One thing really stood out for me from that interview. Dr. Underwood was clearly pleased with my proposal and was prepared to accept me as a graduate student in his program (in the end, I decided not to go to Nottingham and chose to attend Rutgers University to study communication). However, Dr. Underwood had this important piece of advice. There is, in principle, nothing strange or controversial about the subliminal perception hypothesis. It is simply an extension of the established information processing model of attention and memory. However, there is something strange and controversial about the term "subliminal." Dr. Underwood suggested that if I intended to pursue this course of study, I needed to stop using the term "subliminal." He suggested that I used terms like "unattended stimuli" or "implicit cognition" (Underwood, 1996). The word "subliminal," he said, would simply open up a quagmire of misunderstanding that I simply did not need to be involved in. This attitude is echoed by Dixon (1971):

> There evidently is something about subliminal perception which invites confusion. But why? What is there about this hypothesis that it should invite such misconceptions? And what is there about it which should make it so attractive to some as it is abhorrent to others? (Dixon, 1971, p. 5)

There is something other than questions of theory and method at work here. One way to address Dixon's concerns is to turn to the relationship of psychology and communication. When subliminal perception is discussed within the language of the transmission regime of communication, a very different picture appears.

It is clear that the subliminal perception hypothesis brings together all the major themes discussed in this book so far: the invoking of the unconscious; the identification of the limen; the computer metaphor of an objective information processing mechanism in the mind; and, more importantly for us, the issues of malleability of memory and meaning described by Loftus, and Locke's claim that communication is fundamentally imperfect. In Locke's philosophy, the end of communication is the excitation of an idea in the mind of a receiver by the idea in the mind of a sender. The subliminal perception hypothesis suggests that processing of messages can take place at a preconscious level. However, more than this, it seems to suggest that such processing takes place even for messages that are not available to conscious awareness. Further, it seems to imply the possibility of transmitting messages subliminally which can be recognized, processed, and responded to without the person being aware of the presence of that message.

In the heyday of speculations on the nature of the unconscious in the late nineteenth century, much attention was paid to issues like these. Researchers of psychical phenomena addressed the question of direct communication from one mind to another without the intermediate influence of conscious awareness. Such direct communication was called telepathy, and was said to have occurred when "there is reason to suppose that the mind of one human being has affected the mind of another, without speech uttered, or word written, or sign made" (Gurney, Myers, & Podmore, 1886/1970, p. xxxv). In principle, telepathy represents the ideal form of communication because it implies that the unconscious mind of a sender can transmit ideas directly to the unconscious mind of a receiver without the corrupting influence of the intermediate stages of transformation. There would be no need for words. No need for encoding or decoding. You would receive my pure idea without the distorting effects of language identified by Locke and Berkeley. The "mist before our eyes," as Locke put it, would be lifted. The hypothesis of subliminal perception within cognitive psychology is a variation on the claim that the communication of messages can take place without the requirement that a person be consciously aware of the presence of those messages.

The concepts of communication and consciousness are key concepts in understanding the nature of this controversy. Like Loftus's work on memory, Dixon's account of consciousness is of a malleable entity, dependent on prior preconscious forces over which the individual can exercise no control and which, in turn, have the capacity to be influenced by subliminal stimuli. The fear, then, is not in terms of a theoretical challenge to an existing paradigm of information processing. Dixon would never claim subliminal perception to be that, although others might (Marcel, 1983). The controversy is operating at a level more fundamentally human than that. The fear is that our conscious experience, our thoughts and feelings, can be influenced by messages of which we are not, and cannot, be aware. Such fears are reminiscent of the response to hypodermic models of the mass media (see Bineham, 1988; Klapper, 1960), in which indoctrination and propaganda were seen as natural misuses of the new technology. It is reminiscent of the belief in the power of the sender in persuasion research (Hovland, Janis, & Kelley, 1953) and the power of television to inspire violence in children (NIMH, 1982).

Dixon's model of subliminal perception has been read, not as a model of information processing, but as a model of communication. Research into subliminal perception seems to suggest that it is possible to transmit messages at a subliminal level and produce measurable responses in receivers. When subliminal perception is viewed in terms of human information processing, the question to be addressed is: what is the nature of *the system* that produces these responses? This is not controversial. However, when subliminal perception is viewed as a form of communication, the questions of importance become: What kinds of effects can we *produce* with a message transmitted at a subliminal level? Can we predict and control these effects? Can we produce persuasive effects? Can a subliminally transmitted message be effective in influencing a person's ideas, attitudes, or behaviors? As with Loftus's research on long-term memory, Dixon's controversy represents a situation in which the language of communication has come to have a significant impact on the language of psychology, and of how psychology must come to understand its objects of knowledge.

When Communication Informs Psychology

Communication is the "transfer of meaning" has an appealing ring to it. But since none of our receptors is capable of receiving "meaning," the notion of transfer is a flagrantly untenable one. The typical formula, A -- B = X (A "communicates" something to B with X result), is similarly misleading. . . . It is quite observable that the process is neither linear nor algebraic. (Lee Thayer)

In this chapter, I have suggested that there is a close relationship between the language of communication studies and the language of information processing models of cognitive psychology. In their early manifestations, discourses of communication drew upon information processing models to enable them to speak in a scientifically authoritative and legitimate way. Communication was located within psychology, with the result that communication became an end product of a prior system of information processing capabilities. However, as we have seen in the discussions of Loftus's work on memory and Dixon's work on subliminal perception, the principles of information processing have also come to be understood in terms of the discourse of communication.

In 1690, John Locke wrote of the inherent ambiguity and malleability of communication and the impossibility of establishing a direct correspondence between idea, meaning, and symbol. He wrote of the role of an active mental faculty of the human understanding which worked upon stimuli derived from the senses to construct objects of knowledge for consideration by the mind. The machine analogy of the information processing paradigm, however, has significant inadequacies in capturing these qualities. Computers are not agents in the processes they execute and they have no capacity to understand one another's goals. As Shotter (1975) notes, "compared with other organisms, never mind persons, mechanisms are somewhat limited" (p. 62).

John Searle (1984) offers a similar critique of the information processing view of the human individual. The basis of the information processing framework is at first glance quite logical and appealing:

> Thinking is processing information, but information processing is just symbol manipulation. Computers do symbol manipulation. So the best way to study thinking (or . . . cognition) is to study computational symbol manipulating programs, whether they are in computers or in brains. (Searle, 1984, p. 43)

However, Searle (1984) argues that to conceptualize people as machines is inherently invalid because the two systems operate with fundamentally different kinds of information. He points out that machines have the ability to manipulate symbols according to a set of predefined rules, the computer program. For the computer, the symbols are represented as digital signals (on/off combinations) which stand in predefined relationships with each other. The program will tell the system what to do with these signals, specify the relationships between them, but there is no inherent understanding in the system of the meaning of those signals and their relationships. The system is operating purely at a syntactic level of information. Any notion of meaning must lie outside of the system either in the programmer who wrote the program or the operator who interprets it. The system itself knows nothing, in the semantic sense, of what it is doing.

Yet a regime of communication immersed in a discourse of cognitive psychology still takes as its object of study the rules and procedures by which information is manipulated even when a knowledge of those rules and procedures can tell us nothing of the meaning of the information being processed. For Searle (1984), this represents a fundamental mistake. He argues that humans act on the basis of meanings and not formal processing procedures:

> We are told that human beings follow rules, and that computers follow rules. But I want to argue that there is a crucial difference.

In the case of human beings, whenever we follow a rule, we are being guided by the actual content or the meaning of the rule. In the case of human rule following, meanings cause behavior. (Searle, 1984, p. 46)

This problem forms the basis of Shotter's (1975) perspective for the study of human action. Shotter asserts that there is a need to change psychology from the study of rules and procedures to an analysis of the symbolic and intersubjective nature of understandings and how these guide social action (as opposed to behavior). The source of such understandings will lie not in the mechanistic procedures of information processing, but in the social context of a culture. Shotter (1975) believes that:

What has been overlooked in modern psychology, especially in its more extreme mechanistic-behavioristic manifestations as a natural science of behavior, is that man is not simply a being immersed directly in nature but is a being *in a culture* in nature. (p. 13)

Shotter's perspective is not concerned with how a person processes data from an essentially meaningless material environment. Rather it is concerned with how a person comes to understand symbols and meanings in a cultural environment and comes to act on the basis of those understandings. It would include accounts of how people interact, how they create and share meanings and mutually understand them, and how immersion in a culture, the totality of all those meanings, can guide and make sense of human behavior, both for the actor and the observer.

There is a growing recognition within cognitive psychology that a fundamental change is required in the information processing framework as a model of human action and behavior, including communication behavior (see Giorgi, 1970; Harre, Clarke, & De Carlo, 1985; Harre & Secord, 1972; Shotter, 1975, 1984). For example, Shotter (1975) argues that a theoretical framework based on the analogy of machine and engineering systems is inappropriate and misleading for the study of people. Shotter believes that to continue psychology in a meaningful and valid way, it is necessary to adopt an entirely new framework. Such a perspective is discussed at length in Shotter (1975, 1984) and Gauld and Shotter (1977).

A similar realization that an information processing view of communication processes may be limited or even inappropriate is also present in the discourse of communication theorists. For example, Lee Thayer (1979) has argued that the traditional information foundations of communication are simply inappropriate to the study of human behavior and, as a result, the research carried out on the basis of those foundations is highly misleading and ultimately unproductive. As Thayer (1979) points out:

> The ways in which we traditionally and conventionally conceive of communication-those being inadequate and untenable-stand as obstacles to more adequate and more potent ways of conceiving of communication. . . . Those preconceptions, our traditional concepts of communication, are often insidious. "Communication is the 'transfer of meaning'" has an appealing ring to it. But since none of our receptors is capable of receiving "meaning," the notion of transfer is a flagrantly untenable one. The typical formula, A -- B = X (A "communicates" something to B with X result), is similarly misleading. . . . It is quite observable that the process is neither linear nor algebraic. (p. 10)

Thayer (1979) argues that human communication is being forced into a framework which was not designed or intended for it. In the context of the information theory paradigm, communication is always the result, an artifact, of behavior. It does not constitute an object of study in itself. As in the field of cognitive psychology, there is a growing awareness that the prevailing paradigms are failing and that conceptual change is necessary.

One can see from this discussion that the relationship between psychology and communication is not a simple one. Taken at face value as expressed in the descriptions of communication given by my students, the relationship of communication and psychology should be relatively straightforward. Communication is the transmission of ideas from one mind to another. Psychology is the discipline that can describe how the mind does this. But this apparently common sense story is not the only reason why the modern discourses of communication take this psychological line. If one listens to my students, the story they tell is that someone, Claude Shannon maybe, conceived of communication as a sender-message-receiver process and then looked around for appropriate theoretical and methodological tools that would enable him or her to describe and explain this process. Psychology just happened to be there, like a book encountered on a library shelf.

In the preceding chapters, I have attempted to show that the discourse of psychology and communication grew from the same discursive soil, framed by an epistemic discourse of the unthought (Foucault, 1973). The differentiation of an objectified discursive realm for scientific description and experimentation made possible both the modern discourse of psychology and the contemporary discursive regime of communication. Considered in these terms, psychology and communication do not fit together neatly like two pieces of a jigsaw puzzle, much as my students would like them to. Psychologists advocated the rigor and predictability of an information processing system based in a computer metaphor. It offered the promise of generalizable and universal conclusions about the nature of the human mental apparatus. However, Locke's view of communication offered a perspective in which meanings were derived in contexts unique to each individual. A given outcome could not be predicted from any given message and mental processes produced results that were fundamentally ambiguous and subjective. Instead of accounts of communication becoming more like the language of psychology, it seems the opposite is becoming the case; accounts of psychology are becoming more like the language of communication.

Six

Learning to Speak Differently About Communication: *Which Do You Wish?*

"Which do you wish: to see five or to persuade me that you see five?" (O'Brien to Winston Smith)

When pushed, my students' reactions to being asked to reflect at length on "What is communication?" eventually produce expressions of exasperation and frustration. This is not a reaction unique to these considerations of communication. As Ludwig Wittgenstein (1958) remarks, "the questions 'What is length?', 'What is meaning?', 'What is the number one?', etc., produce in us a mental cramp. We feel that we can't point to anything in reply to them and yet ought to point to something" (p. 1).

My students often express the same sentiment as Wittgenstein. They end up with the realization that there is nothing concrete to which they can point to justify their words. Where are the ideas? Where are the interpretations? Where are the neurons and synaptic firings that make all this work? All they can do is invoke the black hole of unconscious information-processing routines and express their faith that the concrete equivalent of their words really exists somewhere. The students quickly realize that our discussion of the question "What is communication?" has led them into a seemingly endless labyrinth of words and terms, all generating other words and terms, but, when all is said and done, no tangible object appears to hang these terms together.

As we have seen, the discursive regime of communication compels my students to consider communication as a function of the mind or the brain. It is there that they see the reality of communication because it is there that they see its cause. A speaker produces the ideas she wishes to convey inside her head. There is a process by which those ideas are encoded. A listener receives the speaker's words and she must "interpret" and "understand" those symbols by some assumed ability of the listener's mind. This assumption is not based on any direct evidence. It is something that just seems natural. As Wittgenstein (1958) remarks, "it seems that there are *certain definite* mental processes bound up with the working of language, processes through which alone language can function" (p. 3). Wittgenstein (1958) continues: "The signs of our language seem dead without these mental processes; and it might seem that the only function of the signs is to induce such processes, and that these are the things we ought really to be interested in" (p. 3).

In this way of talking, communication would seem to be the result of two parts, which Wittgenstein characterizes as the organic and the inorganic. The inorganic part is the physical handling of signs; the production and transmission of signs from one place to another. The organic part refers to the understanding of these signs, and the concomitant processes of interpretation, thinking, and meaning. These latter activities, Wittgenstein (1958) notes, "seem to take place in a queer kind of mechanism, the mind" (p. 3):

> Without a sense, or without the thought, a proposition would be an utterly dead and trivial thing. And further it seems clear that no adding of inorganic signs can make the proposition live. And the conclusion which one draws from this is that what must be added to the dead signs in order to make a live proposition is something immaterial, with properties different from all mere signs. (p. 4)

It is precisely down this road that my students embark in search of that queer kind of mechanism that is immaterial and different from physical signs. As a result, we inevitably get hopelessly lost.

Wittgenstein is also puzzled about this, but not about where the immaterial process can be found, but why we should seek to embark on such a fruitless search in the first place. According to Wittgenstein, our obsession with the queer, mysterious nature of thought is a "puzzlement caused by the mystifying use of our language" (p. 6). It is simply misleading to talk of thinking as a "mental activity." Wittgenstein suggests that a more fruitful way of talking is to say that thinking is essentially the "activity of operating with signs" (p. 6). So, for Wittgenstein, when we write, we are "thinking with our hand." When we speak, we are "thinking with our mouths and larynx." Expressions such as

"we think with our hand,"
"we think with our mouth," or
"we think with a pencil on a piece of paper"

seem strange to us. But we are content to say things like

"we think with our head" or
"we think with our brain."

Why do we prefer the latter expressions to the former?

We are accustomed to speaking about our head as being the locality of our thoughts because the existence of the terms "thinking" and "thought" alongside terms denoting bodily activities such as "writing" or "speaking" (e.g., "I am writing down my thoughts" or "Let me tell you what my thoughts are") make us look for an activity corresponding to the term "thinking." We say things like "the thought is not the same as the sentence." The regime of communication suggests to us that an act of communication begins with the thought which is then encoded into signs. This difference must be "real" because isn't it possible to express the same thought in different ways? Can I not paraphrase the same idea in different sentences? And what about different languages? The same thought sounds very different when it is expressed in English and French. So we can find the sentences. What we need to do next is find the thought that generated the sentence and which precedes and lies beyond it. The thought must be *something*. It cannot be nothing. In these terms, it seems quite reasonable to speak of a "locality" where this "something" can reside. The most common locality is our head or, more specifically, to those certain physiological processes inside our brains which must, somehow, correspond with the thoughts we experience. This is the place where my students invariably end up. They are fishing for terms to describe the nature of this locality and of the relationship between physiological happenings in the brain to thought. They find this very difficult and are content with phrases like "thought takes place in the brain" with no further reflection. This sentence, and others like it, represents the limit of how far they can go.

Some students imagine and speculate that the relationship between physiological brain processes and actual thoughts can be verified in some experimental manner. Maybe we could observe a subject's brain while that subject thinks about something. They envision some high-tech MRI type machine which could display changes in brain activity. You could then correlate the activity to the thoughts reported by the subject. These connections seem tenuous, but are the best they can come up with.

Wittgenstein (1958/1965) posits the following thought experiment created in the days before MRI machines, but the example still holds. Let us say that the subject is the experimenter and she is observing her own brain activity via an MRI display and various EEG readouts. The subject thinks about the price of chips in Sutton-in-Ashfield and observes a corresponding change in the MRI display. Wittgenstein raises the following questions with respect to this situation:

When looking at the MRI display, is the subject/experimenter observing one thing or two things?

Wittgenstein suggests that the subject is observing the correlation of two phenomena. The first phenomena the subject calls "the thought": this is the train of images, sensations, or internal dialogue the subject experiences as "thinking." The second phenomena is "seeing her brain work"; the different levels of activity as recorded by the MRI machine. Both of these phenomena are expressions of thought. The experience of looking at the MRI display itself requires a mental process of recognition and understanding. Indeed, the "thought" being experienced by the subject needs another "thought" which says that what I am currently experiencing is a thought. When the subject observes the MRI display, which "thought" is being reflected in the brain activity displayed? The subject requires a "thought" to experience the "thought." But the question that motivated this study was "Where is the original thought?" Can we see it? I can say "I close my eyes and think of my pet cat." I think of the cat, but how can I think of the thought? The more we reflect on this, the more nonsensical the whole task becomes. Despite this, my students still like to say that "my thoughts are in my head." What I tell them in return is that this expression is *not a description of something real*. It is an expression that justifies a hypothesis and allows people in the world to operate as if thoughts really did exist in this fashion.

Yet the idea of thoughts being things located in the head is a very powerful one, as is the idea that communication begins in people's heads. Students always come back to the idea that words "excite, in the Hearer, exactly the same Idea, they stand for in the Mind of the speaker" (Locke, 1975, p. 478; Essay, III, ix) or that "the word *communication* will be used here in a very broad sense to include all procedures by which one mind may affect another (Weaver, 1949, p. 3).

But these are hypotheses rather than descriptions. The role of mental processes in communication is a hypothesis that is expressed in a particular language with a particular grammar. The hypothesis that "thinking is located in the brain" is a form of speaking and a form of grammar. It is an expression that we use in our everyday speech which has taken on the quality of a real place. Wittgenstein remarks that it is "extremely important to realize how, by misunderstanding the grammar of our expressions, we are led to think of one in particular of these statements as giving the *real* seat of the activity of the mind" (p. 16). The nature of our expressions leads us to believe in a *real* separation of mental content from communication. Wittgenstein warns that we must not be misled by expressions such as "I find it difficult to put my thoughts into words." The separation of thought and language implied here is a metaphor. To say that my words express an idea in our mind suggests we are expressing in words something that has already been expressed, but only in a different thought-language. Communication requires the translation from the mental to the verbal. But without language, how can we understand the thought-language that precedes verbal language? What is it like to experience a thought in its pure, pre-linguistic form? Perhaps the only ones who can truly know are babies who have yet to learn language. Unfortunately, they do not possess the language to report or describe this experience to us. Why do we need a notion of a pre-linguistic language, especially since it is impossible to describe, in language, what this thought-language would be like. It is inconceivable and indescribable, and yet we place it at the center of our conception of the reality of communication. It is like Kant's thing-in-itself, which we know exists, but which we can never experience in and of itself.

Wittgenstein (1958) suggests that we turn away from this search for the unknowable and indescribable. He remarks:

I have been trying in all this to remove the temptation to think there "*must* be" what is called a mental process of thinking, hoping, wishing, believing, etc., independent of the process of expressing a thought, a hope, a wish, etc. (p. 41)

At the present time, the dominant trend is to believe in the reality of mental processes, but we don't have to do this. These expressions create a trap for our thinking about communication, one which eventually pushes us down the dark alley that Wittgenstein describes. Wittgenstein wants us to understand that: "the expression of belief, thought, etc., is just a sentence; - and the sentence has sense only as a member of a system of language; as one expression within a calculus" (p. 42). In talking about communication, we have become hindered by the hypothesis that the meaning of a word resides in something beyond the word. We look for the meaning of a linguistic entity in something that itself is not linguistic, but physical. Wittgenstein does not want to deny that such processes exist, that is not the point of his argument. His claim here is only that we do not need to *postulate* such mental processes in our explanations for how language and communication operates. The word "thought" is something that appears in expressions, in conversations, in acts of speech. To understand "thought," it is not necessary to look for the underlying mental process, but how that word is used in the calculus of a language system. What is its place? What other terms is it related to? In what kinds of expressions and speech acts does it appear? Wittgenstein (1958) concludes that:

> If we are to scrutinize the usages which we make of such words as "thinking," "meaning," "wishing," etc., going through this process rids us of the temptation to look for a particular act of thinking, independent of the act of expressing our thoughts, and stowed away in some particular medium. (p. 43)

How is this scrutiny to take place? And even if we do scrutinize the usages which we make of terms such as "thought," "meaning," and "idea," as I routinely do with my students, how can I be sure that my students are no longer seized by the temptation to believe that an act of thinking is always independent of the act of expressing? I can usually have my students agree, eventually, that my argument that thoughts do not exist makes sense at some level. But this agreement is soon forgotten, and they continue to live their lives according to a discourse which tells them that thoughts and mental processes precede every act of communication. How do we rid the students of this temptation? We have no better model than the character of O'Brien in George Orwell's novel, *1984*.

Confession is Not Betrayal

*Confession is not betrayal. What you say or do doesn't matter;
only feelings matter. If they could make me stop loving you-that
would be the real betrayal. (Winston Smith to Julia)*

Nineteen forty-nine was a watershed year for the contemporary
discursive regime of communication. This year witnessed the publication of
Claude Shannon and Warren Weaver's *The Mathematical Theory of
Communication* which, according to Rogers and Valente (1993), "helped set
off the academic field of communication theory and research" (p. 48).
Nineteen forty-nine also saw the publication of another text that has also
potentially far-reaching implications for the nature and study of human
communication, George Orwell's (1949/1984) *1984*. However, Orwell's
importance lies in the fact that *1984* offers us a way out of the constraints
imposed by a transmission-based regime of communication of the kind
inspired by Shannon and Weaver.

Superficially, it may appear that Orwell's book directly addresses a
transmission conception of communication which is quite consistent with
that inspired by Shannon and Weaver. It is quite appropriate to read *1984*
as a critique of the control and use of mass propaganda by a totalitarian state
symbolized by the face of Big Brother. The Party is the source of all mass
communication technologies and directly controls the content and the means
of communication in an attempt to suppress the thoughts and actions of its
citizens. Expressed in these terms, *1984* would seem to embody Weaver's
concern with communication as a process intended to affect conduct in a
desired way (his level C communication problem). It also speaks a language
similar to that of Norbert Wiener and his association of communication with
control. Orwell's novel also seems to address concerns raised by
Christopher Simpson (1994) in his description of the rise of communication
research as a result of its collaboration with the United States Government's
development of programs to study psychological warfare.

Winston is well aware of the close relationship between
communication and control and the difficulties of communicating his
thoughts within an environment of mass propaganda and the Thought Police.
How can the individual mind maintain its integrity and communicate its
thoughts to other minds in such a place? Winston is also well aware of the
problem of communicating thoughts effectively. His job at the Ministry of
Truth required the rewriting of newspaper copy to conform to the political
and ideological needs of the Party. Sitting in his room writing his secret and
illegal diary, Winston thinks:

For whom, it suddenly occurred to him to wonder, was he writing this diary? For the future, for the unborn. His mind hovered for a moment round the doubtful date on the page, and then fetched up with a bump against the Newspeak word *doublethink*. For the first time the magnitude of what he had undertaken came home to him. How could you communicate with the future? It was of its nature impossible. Either the future would resemble the present in which case it would not listen to him, or it would be different from it, and his predicament would be meaningless. (p. 10)

Such reflections make Winston a hero for us in our contemporary transmission regime of communication. He recognizes that he must get beyond actual words and messages to the reality of the ideas that produced them. He knows full well that communication in *1984* is not meant to enlighten or reveal. Like John Locke, Winston is fully cognizant of the fundamental premise that communication "casts a mist before our eyes." Nowhere is this mist more apparent, and more beautifully described, than in *1984*. We see Winston as a hero because he is determined to peer through the manipulation of Locke's mist and to rebel against the control of communication.

Winston is also the hero of the transmission regime because he is described by Orwell as a physically fragile man, but nevertheless strong in heart and determined to cling on to his individual thoughts and feelings. For Winston, "anything that hinted at corruption always filled him with a wild hope. Who knew? Perhaps the Party was rotten under the surface, its cult of strenuousness and self-denial simply a sham concealing inequity" (p. 104). For Winston, like my students describing communication, reality always lies below the surface. The reality of communication must be something other than its appearance. If it were not, then there would be nothing to hope or live for. The reality had to be something different. In their first sexual encounter somewhere in the countryside outside of London, Winston talks with Julia:

"Listen. The more men you've had, the more I love you. Do you understand that?"

"Yes, perfectly."

"I hate purity, I hate goodness. I don't want any virtue to exist anywhere. I want everyone to be corrupt to the bones."

"Well then, I ought to suit you, dear. I'm corrupt to the bones."

"You like doing this? I don't mean simply me; I mean the thing in itself?"

"I adore it."

That was above all what he wanted to hear. Not merely the love of one person, but the animal instinct, the simple undifferentiated desire; that was the force that would tear the Party to pieces."

(Orwell, 1949/1984, pp. 104-105)

Winston understands that terms such as "goodness" and "purity" do not describe objective realities, but are words that are defined and used by the Party according to their own interests and purposes. Winston wants to get back to the "animal instinct" and the "simple undifferentiated desire" that lies beyond language. This realm is beyond the control of the Party, or so he believes.

Such undifferentiated experiences are not limited to the raw animal instincts of sexual attraction and desire. Winston believes it is also contained in the reality of deep inner feelings, such as the love one person can feel for another. Winston wants to separate the reality of his love for Julia as it "exists" inside him from any expression of love that is sanctioned and controlled by the Party. Winston is well aware of the fact that his feelings for Julia are not tolerated by the Party. He knew that:

The aim of the Party was not merely to prevent men and women from forming loyalties which it might not be able to control. Its real, undeclared purpose was to remove all pleasure from the sexual act. Not love so much as eroticism was the enemy, inside marriage as well as outside it. (Orwell, 1949/1984, p. 57)

Winston knows that if his relationship with Julia is discovered by the Thought Police, he will be tortured and forced to renounce his feelings for Julia. Even with this terrible knowledge, Winston clings to his differentiation between what he thinks and what he says, between real feeling and linguistic expression. He believes that his love for Julia exists in a place beyond language and the reach of the Party:

"If you mean confessing," she said, "we shall do that, right enough. Everybody always confesses. You can't help it. They torture you."

115

"I don't mean confessing. Confession is not betrayal. What you say or do doesn't matter; only feelings matter. If they could make me stop loving you-that would be the real betrayal."

She thought it over. "They can't do that," she said finally. "It's the one thing they can't do. They can make you say anything-*anything*-but they can't make you believe it. They can't get inside you."

"No," he said a little more hopefully, "no; that's quite true. They can't get inside you. If you can *feel* that staying human is worth while, even when it can't have any result whatever, you've beaten them." (Orwell, 1949/1984, pp. 137-138)

The remarks of Winston and Julia reflect Wittgenstein's argument that since we have terms such as "love" and "feeling," then these terms should refer to objects that exist somewhere in their own right, independent and distinct from the language used to express them. John Locke made the same point. Since ideas were separate from language, one could escape the political and ideological constraints of a tyrannical government.

Yet, as those of who have read *1984* are well aware, there is another side to this novel that is of equal, if not more, importance than Winston's belief in the authenticity of real inner feelings and ideas. In many respects, Winston's beliefs and actions can be seen as a foil, a straw man, for *1984*'s real protagonist, O' Brien. O'Brien is a member of the inner party who interrogates Winston after Winston is arrested by the Thought Police for various acts of subversion against the Party. The final third of *1984* details Winston's attempts to maintain his belief in the reality of autonomous thought and feeling in the face of O'Brien's demonstrations that such beliefs are nonsense and the result of delusions. O'Brien plays a role similar to that of Wittgenstein who, through his analysis of terms such as "thought," "idea," and "feeling," can only conclude that the only reality that can exist for us is that reality constructed and mediated through language.

The dialogue between O'Brien and Winston mirrors in many ways the dialogues I have with my students immersed in their transmission regime of communication. We travel down discursive pathways looking for the reality that props up the language of "idea," "thought," and "feeling," only to find more and more language. Like my students, Winston's conception of the real reality gets pushed farther and farther back behind the contingencies of language. In the end, the only reality Winston can appeal to is a metaphysical one-the "spirit of man." It is the only expression he has left to combat O'Brien. Winston tells O'Brien: "I know that you will fail. There is something in the universe-I don't know, some spirit, some principle - that you will never overcome . . . The spirit of Man" (Orwell, 1949/1984, p. 222). O'Brien has a very different picture of the reality facing Winston: "If you want a picture of the future, imagine a boot stamping on a human face-forever" (Orwell, 1949/1984, p. 220).

Yet even deep in the vaults in the Ministry of Love, we are still encouraged to think that Winston's belief in autonomous thought and feeling can prevail. Winston plots one last act of subversion-to think as an individual at the moment the executioner's bullet enters his brain:

> One day they would decide to shoot him. You could not tell when it would be happen, but a few seconds beforehand it should be possible to guess. It was always from behind, walking down a corridor. Ten seconds would be enough. In that time the world inside him could turn over. And then suddenly, without a word uttered, without a check in his step, without the changing of a line in his face-suddenly the camouflage would be down and bang! would go the batteries of his hatred. Hatred would fill him like an enormous roaring flame. And almost in the same instant bang! would go the bullet, too late, or too early. They would have blown his brain to pieces before they could reclaim it. The heretical thought would be unpublished, unrepented, out of their reach forever. They would have blown a hole in their own perfection. To die hating them, that was freedom. (Orwell, 1949/1984, p. 231)

Surely Winston, and the transmission regime of communication, will prevail in the end. To validate the existence of autonomous individual thought at the moment of death would be Winston's victory over the Party and the validation of the transmission regime of communication. The separation of thought from word would triumph in the face of the Party's attempts to obliterate the distinction. Winston's victory would be the victory of the individual and of the individual's privileged place within the transmission regime of communication.

However, by the end of the book, it becomes very clear that Winston does not prevail. It is O'Brien and the Party that claims victory. Winston does betray Julia, the Party does get inside him, and Winston does submit his individuality. O'Brien's world view wins out over Winston's; the will of the Party does indeed supercede the will of the individual. What is important in this novel is not Winston's all too familiar position. To see Winston prevail and the Party crumble against Winston's "real feelings" would be as predictable as the ending of the latest James Bond movie. What strikes us is the manner and legitimacy of O'Brien's victory, and the insights it has to offer into the regime of communication in the present. These insights far transcend the transmission concepts of control and propaganda. They concern the creation of individuals and the creation of worlds in which those individuals can live.

How Many Fingers Am I Holding Up, Winston?

In the final third of *1984*, O'Brien will violently attack Winston's discourse of individual thought and feeling using extreme physical torture. However, his stated goal is *not* to teach Winston some new point of view which he can place above his previous view by the threat of pain:

> "And why do you imagine that we bring people to this place?"
> "To make them confess."
> "No, that is not the reason. Try again."
> "To punish them."
> "No!" exclaimed O'Brien. His voice had changed extraordinarily, and his face had become both stern and animated. "No! Not merely to extract your confession, nor to punish you. Shall I tell you why we have brought you here? To cure you! To make you sane! Will you understand, Winston, that no one whom we bring to this place ever leaves our hands uncured? We are not interested in those stupid crimes that you have committed. The Party is not interested in the overt act: the thought is all we care about. We do not merely destroy our enemies; we change them. Do you understand what I mean by that?" (Orwell, 1949/1984, pp. 208-209)

The problem O'Brien faces with Winston is the same problem I face with my students trapped within this regime of communication. It is not enough to have them "confess" in papers or on tests their understanding of our discussions of communication and the limits of their language. Indeed, they can articulate quite clearly that their knowledge of communication is bound together by a particular vocabulary and a grammatical logic. Yet they persist in holding Winston's attitude when he tells Julia "What you say or do doesn't matter; only feelings matter . . . They can't get inside you." The students tell me about how their knowledge of communication is created and bound by language, but they don't believe it in any real sense. They believe insofar as it will enable them to do well in the course and earn a good grade. But beyond the classroom and beyond the context of our conversations, communication really *is* a process of transmission. Again, the thoughts of Winston provide their model:

> The Party told you to reject the evidence of your eyes and ears. It was their final, most essential command. His heart sank as he thought of the enormous power arrayed against him, the ease with which any Party intellectual would overthrow him in debate, the subtle arguments which he would not be able to understand, much less answer. And yet he was in the right! They were wrong and he was right. The obvious, the silly, and the true had got to be defended. Truisms are true, hold on to that! The solid world exists, its laws do not change. Stones are hard, water is wet, objects unsupported fall towards the earth's center. With the feeling that he was speaking to O'Brien, and also that he was setting forth an important axiom, he wrote:
>
> *Freedom is the freedom to say that two plus two makes four. If that is granted, all else follows.*
>
> (Orwell, 1949/1984, p. 69)

Even if we adopt a new framework to describe communication, we unwittingly use the language of the old, "for everywhere one runs into the old threads, and each one pushes conversation and thought back a little way toward the established pattern" (Reddy, 1979, p. 297). For example, if I set a reading for a class, it is so natural to ask the students "What did you get out this reading?" or "What do you understand by this?" or "What did the author mean by this?" How else are we to discuss these everyday classroom activities? Reddy remarks that: "if you try to avoid all obvious conduit metaphor expressions in your usage, you are nearly struck dumb when communication becomes the topic" (p. 299).

To understand a discourse of communication beyond the Lockean/unconscious/information-processing world view requires that we rip down the structures within which we have been so thoroughly socialized. O'Brien's interrogation and torture of Winston is the only way to break through regimes like this. With students, the "reality" of the transmission view snaps back into focus as soon as the class ends.

"Oh that was an interesting discussion," they say, "but we all know what communication is like really."

119

Orwell, through O'Brien, represents how far I would need to take my discussion with the students to prevent this snapping back. In my interrogations of the students' beliefs, we generally stop when the language runs out. When O'Brien holds up four fingers and asks Winston how many fingers he is holding up, Winston replies "four." For Winston, what more is there to be said? His answer represents the appropriate correspondence between what he sees and what he says. But O'Brien, to Winston's horror, pushes on into a realm where Winston's language is no longer adequate to carry on the conversation. How is he supposed to answer the second time? What is he supposed to say? What is the appropriate next response in this bizarre language game?

> "Do you remember," he went on, "writing in your diary, 'Freedom is the freedom to say that two plus two make four'?"
> "Yes," said Winston.
> O'Brien held up his left hand, its back toward Winston, with the thumb hidden and the four fingers extended.
> "How many fingers am I holding up, Winston?"
> "Four."
> "And if the Party says that it is not four but five-then how many?"
> "Four."
> The word ended in a gasp of pain. The needle on the dial had shot up to fifty-five. The sweat had sprung out all over Winston's body. The air tore into his lungs and issued again in deep groans which even by clenching his teeth he could not stop. O'Brien watched him, the four fingers still extended. He drew back the lever. This time the pain was only slightly eased.
> "How many fingers, Winston?"
> "Four."
> The needle went up to sixty.
> "How many fingers, Winston?"
> "Four! Four! What else can I say? Four!"
> The needle must have risen again, but he did not look at it. The heavy, stern face and the four fingers filled his vision. The fingers stood up before his eyes like pillars, enormous, blurry, and seeming to vibrate, but unmistakably four.
> "How many fingers, Winston?"
> "Four! Stop it, stop it! How can you go on? Four! Four!"
> "How many fingers, Winston?"

"Five! Five! Five!"

"No, Winston, that is no use. You are lying. You still think there are four. How many fingers, please?"

"Four! Five! Four! Anything you like. Only stop it, stop the pain!"

Abruptly he was sitting up with O'Brien's arm round his shoulders. He had perhaps lost consciousness for a few seconds. The bonds that had held his body down were loosened. He felt very cold, he was shaking uncontrollably, his teeth were chattering, the tears were rolling down his cheeks. For a moment he clung to O'Brien like a baby, curiously comforted by the heavy arm round his shoulders. He had the feeling that O'Brien was his protector, that the pain was something that came from outside, from some other source, and that it was O'Brien who would save him from it.

"You are a slow learner, Winston," said O'Brien, gently.

"How can I help it?" he blubbered. "How can I help seeing what is in front of my eyes? Two and two are four."

"Sometimes, Winston. Sometimes they are five. Sometimes they are three. Sometimes they are all of them at once. You must try harder. It is not easy to become sane."

He laid Winston down on the bed. The grip on his limbs tightened again, but the pain had ebbed away and the trembling had stopped, leaving him merely weak and cold. O'Brien motioned with his head to the man in the white coat, who had stood immobile throughout the proceedings. The man in the white coat bent down and looked closely into Winston's eyes, felt his pulse, laid an ear against his chest, tapped here and there; then he nodded to O'Brien.

"Again," said O'Brien.

The pain flowed into Winston's body. The needle must be at seventy, seventy-five. He had shut his eyes this time. He knew that the fingers were still there, and still four. All that mattered was somehow to stay alive until the spasm was over. He had ceased to notice whether he was crying out or not. The pain lessened again. He opened his eyes. O'Brien had drawn back the lever.

"How many fingers, Winston?"

"Four. I suppose there are four. I would see five if I could. I am trying to see five."

"Which do you wish: to persuade me that you see five, or really to see them?"

"Really to see them."

"Again," said O'Brien.

Perhaps the needle was at eighty-ninety. Winston could only intermittently remember why the pain was happening. Behind the screwed-up eyeballs a forest of fingers seemed to be moving in a sort of dance, weaving in and out, disappearing behind one another and reappearing again. He was trying to count them, he could not remember why. He knew only that it was impossible to count them, and that this was somehow due to the mysterious identity between five and four. The pain died down again. When he opened his eyes it was to find that he was still seeing the same thing. Innumerable fingers, like moving trees, were still streaming past in either direction, crossing and recrossing. He shut his eyes again.

"How many fingers am I holding up, Winston?"

"I don't know. I don't know. You will kill me if you do that again. Four, five, six - in all honesty I don't know."

"Better," said O'Brien.

(Orwell, 1949/1984, pp. 206-208)

O'Brien does not stop when the language runs out. He pushes on further, beyond the limits of language, beyond the limits of perception and sensory input, beyond the obviousness of memory, free will, and autonomous individuals. What I need to do is take up the techniques of O'Brien with my students. It is for them to persuade me that they see five fingers. When O'Brien asks Winston to tell him his true feelings toward Big Brother, Winston replies "I hate him." O'Brien replies: "You hate him. Good. Then the time has come for you to take the last step. You must love Big Brother. It is not enough to obey him; you must love him" (Orwell, 1949/1984, p. 232). It is not enough for the students to tell me that they know that the transmission view is a regime of communication constructed from a particular way of talking. They also have to believe it.

The Cartesian Whirlpool

So serious are the doubts into which I have been thrown as a result of yesterday's meditation that I can neither put them out of my mind nor see any way of resolving them. It feels as if I have fallen unexpectedly into a deep whirlpool which tumbles me around so that I can neither stand on the bottom nor swim up to the top. (Rene Descartes)

How is it possible to go beyond the transmission regime of communication to the extent advocated by O'Brien? The first step to cure my students is to have them doubt everything they think they know about it. In the classroom setting, I try, through discussion, to have the students doubt they have ideas, thoughts, or memories. It seems a very bizarre notion at first, but certainly not as bizarre as O'Brien asking Winston how many fingers he was holding up.

"So," I say, "tell me. What you are thinking at this moment?"

I generally get blank looks at this question.

"Come on, tell me what you're thinking about."

After a period of quiet, a student will usually raise her hand.

"I'm thinking about what to make for dinner."

"Really?" I say. "Are you really thinking about dinner, or are you just saying that in response to my question?"

(Which do you wish: to see five or to persuade me that you see five?)

Sometimes I ask them about their memories.

"Tell me your earliest memory," I say.

I get some stories about sitting on mother's knee, or a birthday party.

"Where do these memories exist?" I ask. "Did you access them like a computer reads data from a hard drive? Could you hear the drive motor whir as you found the memory you wanted? Or does the memory you just recounted to me exist solely in the story you told me in response to my question?"

My goal in all of these questions is to try and introduce doubt into the accounts students give of how they think or how they remember. I want them to ask themselves:

"Suppose thoughts and memories don't exist in the form my accounts tell me they exist? Suppose they exist in some other form? Or maybe they don't exist at all?"

I am asking my students to engage in a form of radical Cartesian doubt. Rene Descartes sought to doubt everything until he could find something that could not be doubted, even if this was the proposition that everything was doubtful. Descartes (1641/1984) writes:

> I will suppose then, that everything is spurious. I will believe that my memory tells me lies, and that none of the things that it reports ever happened. I have no senses. Body, shape, extension, movement and place are chimeras. So what remains true? Perhaps just the one fact that nothing is certain. (p. 16)

For example, Descartes doubted the reliability of written records and of what these records state about the nature of the world. If Descartes could demonstrate as false just one fact in the teachings of his mentors, then he felt justified in calling into question the whole enterprise. Descartes (1637/1960) writes:

> From my childhood I lived in a world of books, and since I was taught that by their help I could gain a clear and assured knowledge of everything useful in life, I was eager to learn from them. But as soon as I finished the course of studies which usually admits one to the ranks of the learned, I changed my opinions completely. For I found myself saddled with so many doubts and errors that I seemed to have gained nothing in trying to educate myself unless it was to discover more and more fully how ignorant I am. (p. 5)

In the society of *1984*, Winston is made to doubt the truth of any and all written documents. He is well aware of the Party's control and manipulation of the press through his own work in the Ministry of Truth. How is Winston to trust any text or record produced by the Party? Winston explains in a conversation with Julia (Orwell, 1949/1984, p. 128):

> "Do you realize that the past, starting from yesterday, has been actually abolished? If it survives anywhere, it's in a few solid objects with no words attached to them, like that lump of glass there. Already we know almost literally nothing about the Revolution and the years before the Revolution. Every record has been destroyed or rewritten, every picture has been repainted, every statue and street and building has been renamed, every date has been altered. And that process is continuing day by day and minute by minute. History has

stopped. Nothing exists except an endless present in which the Party is always right. I *know*, of course, that the past is falsified, but it would never be possible for me to prove it, even when I did the falsification myself. After the thing is done, no evidence ever remains. The only evidence is inside my own mind, and I don't know with any certainty that any other human being shares my memories."

The control of all published writing leads Winston to doubt not only the truth and validity of documents, but also the contents of his own memories which are grounded in all the things he has read or been told. O'Brien reinforces these doubts during the interrogation. O'Brien produces a photograph and presents it to Winston:

An oblong slip of newspaper had appeared between O'Brien's fingers. For perhaps five seconds it was within the angle of Winston's vision. It was a photograph, and there was no question of its identity. It was *the* photograph. It was another copy of the photograph of Jones, Aaronson, and Rutherford at the Party function in New York, which he had chanced upon eleven years ago and promptly destroyed. For only an instant it was before his eyes, then it was out of sight again. But he had seen it, unquestionably he had seen it! He made a desperate, agonizing effort to wrench the top half of his body free. It was impossible to move so much as a centimeter in any direction. All he wanted was to hold the photograph in his fingers again, or at least to see it.

"It exists!" he cried.

"No," said O'Brien.

He stepped across the room. There was a memory hole in the opposite wall. O'Brien lifted the grating. Unseen, the frail slip of paper was whirling away on the current of warm air; it was vanishing in a flash of flame. O'Brien turned away from the wall.

"Ashes," he said. "Not even identifiable ashes. Dust. It does not exist. It never existed."

"But it did exist! It does exist! It exists in memory. I remember it. You remember it."

"I do not remember it," said O'Brien.

Winston's heart sank. That was doublethink. He had a feeling of deadly helplessness. If he could have been certain that O'Brien was lying, it would not have seemed to matter. But it was perfectly possible that O'Brien had really forgotten the photograph. And if so, then already he would have forgotten his denial of remembering it, and forgotten the act of forgetting. How could one be so sure that it was simple trickery? Perhaps that lunatic dislocation of the mind could really happen: that was the thought that defeated him. (Orwell, 1949/1984, pp. 203-204)

Winston is slowly coming to the realization that perhaps there is something more to O'Brien's arguments. O' Brien constantly tells Winston to look inwards rather than outwards; that the problems he thinks he sees are not the result of devious machinations of the Party but rather creations of Winston's own deranged mind. O'Brien tells Winston:

You know perfectly well what is the matter with you. You have known it for years, though you have fought against the knowledge. You are mentally deranged. You suffer from a defective memory. You are unable to remember real events, and you persuade yourself that you remember other events which never happened. (p. 203)

As Winston fights against these arguments, O'Brien tells him that "even now, I am well aware, you are clinging to your disease under the impression that it is a virtue" (Orwell, 1949/1984, p. 203). O'Brien even tells Winston that "your mind appeals to me. It resembles my own mind except that you happen to be insane" (Orwell, 1949/1984, p. 213). But Winston is forced to respond:

"But how can you stop people remembering things?" cried Winston, again momentarily forgetting the dial. "It is involuntary. It is outside oneself. How can you control memory? You have not controlled mine!" (Orwell, 1949/1984, p. 205)

But O'Brien argues otherwise:

"On the contrary," he said, "*you* have not controlled it. That is what has brought you here. You are here because you have failed in humility, in self-discipline. You would not make the act of submission which is the price of sanity. You have preferred to be a lunatic, a minority of one. Only the disciplined mind can see reality, Winston. You believe reality is something objective external, existing in its own right. You also believe that the nature of reality is self-evident. When you delude yourself into thinking that you see something, you assume that everybody else sees the same thing as you. But I tell you, Winston, that reality is not external. Reality exists in the human mind, and nowhere else." (Orwell, 1949/1984, p. 205)

O'Brien will systematically lead Winston down this path of radical doubt. Like Descartes, O'Brien will destroy all former opinions in order to leave those truths which are indubitable, and which, of course, conform to the will of the Party. A key maxim of Descartes's method is stated as follows:

A third maxim was always to seek to conquer myself rather than fortune, to change my desires rather then the established order, and generally to believe that nothing except our thoughts is wholly under our control. (Descartes, 1637/1960, p. 20)

Descartes language of "destroying" former opinions and "conquering" himself in order to reach the clear and the distinct captures the essence of O'Brien's project. In their extended torture session, O'Brien tells Winston: "We shall crush you down to the point from which there is no coming back . . . You will be hollow. We shall squeeze you empty, and then we shall fill you with ourselves." (Orwell, 1949/1984, p. 211)

Do It To Julia!

"But what is it, what is it? How can I do it if I don't know what it is?" (Winston Smith)

In his analysis of the conversation between O'Brien and Winston, Richard Rorty (1989) points out:

O'Brien reminds us that human beings who have been socialized-socialized in any language, any culture-do share a capacity which other animals lack. They can all be given a special kind of pain: They can all be humiliated by the forcible tearing down of the particular structures of language and belief in which they were socialized (or which they pride themselves on having formed for themselves). (p. 177)

Rorty (1989) argues that the worst thing you can do to somebody is not to make her scream in agony but to use that agony in such a way that even when the agony is over, she cannot reconstitute herself. She cannot get back to the view she held before, just as my students do. O'Brien needs to get Winston to do and say things, and, if possible, believe and desire things, which later he will be unable to cope with having done or thought. O'Brien seeks to unmake Winston's world by making it impossible for him to use language to describe what he has been.

This goal is the reason why O'Brien goes to such extreme lengths to have Winston state that he holds up five fingers instead of four. Getting Winston to deny a belief or a perception for no reason is the first step in making him incapable of having a sense of self. Winston is unable to give a reason for this belief that fits together with his other beliefs. For example, consider the following exchange when O'Brien offers Winston the opportunity to ask him a few questions. Winston asks:

> "Does Big Brother exist?"
> "Of course he exists. The Party exists. Big Brother is the embodiment of the Party."
> "Does he exist in the same way as I exist?"
> "You do not exist," said O'Brien. (Orwell, 1949/1984, p. 214)

Winston recoils from O'Brien's statement. Again, O'Brien pushes Winston into regions where his language is insufficient to cope. Winston struggles to rationalize O'Brien's statement that he does not exist as "only a play on words" (p. 214), but does not have the language to do so. Winston reflects:

> Did not the statement, "You do not exist," contain a logical absurdity? But what use was it to say so? His mind shriveled as he thought of the unanswerable, mad arguments with which O'Brien would demolish him. (Orwell, 1949/1984, p. 214)

Faced with total immersion in O'Brien's discourse, Winston's own discourse becomes irrational. This is not because Winston's discourse has lost contact with reality. Winston is not able to speak in ways that make sense. O'Brien is making it very clear that everything Winston believed about the world and himself is nonsense, the product of a deranged mind. Winston does not possess the language to rationalize otherwise, even to the point of justifying his own existence.

But there is one last reality that Winston clings to throughout the entirety of his ordeal with O'Brien; his love for Julia and his belief that it exists deep within himself, beyond the reach of O'Brien and the Party. The distinction between feeling and language is a cornerstone of the transmission regime of communication. Feelings are pre-linguistic, like Locke's simple ideas. They are experienced directly and authentically, without the mediation of language and, therefore, the tampering of the Party. The belief in an objective realm of emotion unique to each individual is part of the justification of our conception that we exist as unique individuals. It drives our narrative that communication comes from inside and is an expression of these unique selves. All the communication in the world cannot change this.

O'Brien recognizes the strength of this final belief, just as I recognize it in my students. To give up the discourse of the deep interior would be to give up the discourse of the individual self. No one is going to do this without a fight, and O'Brien is well aware of this:

> "We have beaten you, Winston. We have broken you up. You have seen what your body is like. Your mind is in the same state. I do not think there can be much pride left in you. You have been kicked and flogged and insulted, you have screamed with pain, you have rolled on the floor in your own blood and vomit. You have whimpered for mercy, you have betrayed everybody and everything. Can you think of a single degradation that has not happened to you?"
>
> Winston had stopped weeping, though the tears were still oozing out of his eyes. He looked up at O'Brien.
>
> "I have not betrayed Julia," he said.
>
> O'Brien looked down at him thoughtfully. "No," he said, "no; that is perfectly true. You have not betrayed Julia." (Orwell, 1949/1984, p. 225)

Throughout his ordeal in the Ministry of Love, Winston has always had a discourse of last resort with which to realize his actions of confession and betrayal and keep his belief in his deep interior intact. He said and did the things he did because of the fear and the physical infliction of pain. "'You did it!' sobbed Winston. 'You reduced me to this state'" (Orwell, 1949/1984, p. 225). It is this language of rationalization that O'Brien will attack with the most unimaginable horrors at his disposal.

> "By itself," he said, "pain is not always enough. There are occasions when a human being will stand out against pain, even to the point of death. But for everyone there is something unendurable - something that cannot be contemplated. Courage and cowardice are not involved. If you are falling from a height it is not cowardly to clutch at a rope. If you have come from deep water it is not cowardly to fill your lungs with air. It is merely an instinct which cannot be disobeyed. It is the same with the rats. For you, they are unendurable. They are a form of pressure that you cannot withstand, even if you wish to. You will do what is required of you." (Orwell, 1949/1984, p. 234)

Winston is now at the very limits of what he can say to appease O'Brien. In past conversations, Winston has reported he can see five fingers instead of four. He can agree with O'Brien that the photograph of Jones, Aaronson, and Rutherford never existed. But in this conversation, the next move is unknown to Winston, and the consequences will be catastrophic. Faced with the prospect of having a cage containing two starving rats placed over his face, Winston is at a complete and total loss as to what to say or do to prevent this horror. He screams in anguish:

> "But what is it, what is it? How can I do it if I don't know what it is?" (Orwell, 1949/1984, p. 234)

Winston has run out of moves and O'Brien carries on regardless, setting the cage on Winston's head, preparing to push the levers that will let the rats loose upon his face. Orwell describes the building and sheer intensity of Winston's fear. All at once, Winston knew what he had to say. He knew the last avenue of language left to him:

> For an instant he was insane, a screaming animal. Yet he came out of the blackness clutching an idea. There was one and only one way to save himself. He must interpose another human being, the *body* of another human being, between himself and the rats. (Orwell, 1949/1984, p. 235)

As O'Brien prepares to press the lever that will release the rats on to his face, Winston experiences a tiny fragment of hope: "he had suddenly understood that in the whole world there was just *one* person to whom he could transfer his punishment-*one* body that he could thrust between himself and the rats. And he was shouting frantically, over and over:" (Orwell, 1949/1984, p. 235). And so comes the most poignant and crucial words of Orwell's novel; the words that, once uttered, Winston can never rationalize:

> "Do it to Julia! Do it to Julia! Not me! Julia! I don't care what you do to her. Tear her face off, strip her to the bones. Not me! Julia! Not me!" (Orwell, 1949/1984, p. 236)

Winston might be able to construct a narrative in which believing he saw five fingers made sense to him. The idea that he was temporarily irrational due to electro-shock therapy and torture would certainly keep his sense of a real inner sense intact. But the statement and his belief that he wanted to "Do it to Julia!" is not one he can weave a story around. With the cage on his face, and the rats screeching in his ears, Winston was forced to watch himself go to pieces and at the same time know he could never pick those pieces up again.

O'Brien causes Winston pain in order to force Winston into realizing that he has become incoherent. In O'Brien's world, Winston can no longer use language to sustain his own view of himself as an autonomous individual with his own memories, mental processes, and ideas. The story he had of himself no longer made sense. There is no world in which Winston can picture himself living because there is no legitimate vocabulary in which he could tell a coherent story about himself. For Winston, the one sentence he could not utter sincerely and still be able to put himself back together was "Do it to Julia!" Once one discovers the key sentence and the key thing, O'Brien could tear a mind apart and put it together in new shapes of his own choosing.

After the horror of the Ministry of Love, Winston is released and sitting in the Chestnut Café:

> "They can't get inside you," [Julia] had said. But they could get inside you. "What happens to you here is *forever*," O'Brien had said. That was a true word. There were things, your own acts, from which you could not recover. Something was killed in your breast; burnt out, cauterized out. (Orwell, 1949/1984, p. 239)

Julia enters the café and they have the following conversation:

"Sometimes," she said, "they threaten you with something-something you can't stand up to, can't even think about. And then you say, 'Don't do it to me, do it to somebody else, do it to so-and-so.' And perhaps you might pretend, afterwards, that it was only a trick and that you just said it to make them stop and didn't really mean it. But that isn't true. At the time when it happens you do mean it. You think there is no other way of saving yourself, and you're quite ready to save yourself that way. You *want* it to happen to the other person. You don't give a damn what they suffer. All you care about is yourself." (Orwell, 1949/1984, p. 240)

For both Winston and Julia, the illusion of the deep interior is gone. Both realize that their deepest inner feelings are kept alive only in language. In the world of actions, pain, and survival, the deep interior can be discarded once its value has been destroyed.

Did O'Brien really brainwash Winston? Did he make Winston believe something against his will? Not really. O'Brien carried through Wittgenstein's project by detaching terms as "thought," "memory," and "self" from a sense of reality. Such terms simply did not make sense in the new discourse O'Brien was advocating. O'Brien did not use language to influence Winston's mind. He gave Winston a new way of using language whereby the term "mind" simply made no sense.

To get beyond the contemporary discursive regime of communication, we will have to do something similar. O'Brien was able to shatter, fragment, and make incoherent Winston's discourse of the autonomous mind and the individual self. To understand ourselves as beings immersed in a regime of communication, we will have to do something equally as drastic. To understand communication *as* discourse, it is Orwell who shows us the way.

Seven

A Semiotic and a Phenomenological Discourse of Communication:
The Author Should Die

The author should die once he has finished writing. So as not to trouble the path of the text. (Umberto Eco)

I argued in chapter six that the character of Winston Smith in Orwell's (1949) *1984* was a true adherent to the transmission regime of communication. It was only by means of the most extreme and cruel methods that O'Brien was able to break the hold of the transmission regime on Winston's way of speaking about himself and his relationship to the world and to realize that his discourse of individual "thoughts," "memories," and "feelings" was incoherent and ultimately meaningless. If, like O'Brien, I am to render the transmission regime of communication incoherent for you, the reader, I must also go on the offensive and employ the most extreme measures. *To this end, I have decided that it is necessary to kill myself.*

The discourse of the transmission regime of communication hinges on the premise that communication is a process whereby a message travels from the mind of the sender to the mind of the receiver. Such a proposition is considered by many to be a simple truism. Following O'Brien, this is the truism that must be attacked in order for the edifice to fall. To do this, I must

133

be able to make you seriously address the following questions: Is it possible to articulate a theory of communication that:

- Makes no reference to the individual mind?

- Is not based in the fundamental differentiation of words and ideas proposed by John Locke in 1690?

- Does not talk of communication in terms of matching the ideas of a sender with the ideas of a receiver?

At first glance, such questions may seem absurd. But if you take a moment to think about it, you will find that such a manner of speaking about communication is not far away from your everyday experience. For example, consider what you are doing at this very moment as you read this book. In understanding this text, do you worry that the "ideas" forming in your mind are the same or similar ones in the mind of the author who wrote it? How could you ever know that this is the case? By what criteria can you judge the fit of your interpretation with the author's original intentions? I suppose you could call and ask me what I thought, but by the time this book reaches publication, distribution, and finally makes its way into your hands, my memory of those original intentions may be long gone. Even if they are not, it would take some considerable effort of reconstruction on my part to come up with my interpretation of what those ideas were at that time. I could give you my interpretation of this text as it stands today (i.e., at the same time you are reading it), but wouldn't that also be just another attempt to derive an original idea whose time has long past?

It does not take much critical self-reflection to realize that the notion of communication as a process of "matching ideas" is not an entirely successful way of understanding what is happening when you read this text. Indeed, this way of articulating the situation can be considered an impediment to understanding. Semiotician Umberto Eco believes that authors do not really matter at all. He writes: "I'll tell you at once that I really couldn't care less about the empirical author of a narrative text (or, indeed, of any text)" (1994, p. 11) and that "the author should die once he has finished writing. So as not to trouble the path of the text" (1983, p. 7). This is why I volunteered to "kill myself" at the beginning of this chapter, to foreground my irrelevance to your act of reading and understanding.

What we need to do is either (a) identify or (b) create a discourse in which we can articulate the relationship between the *text and the reader* rather than the *author and the reader* (the sender and the receiver). If we can talk about communication this way, and still make sense, then maybe it will be possible, as Peters (1989) suggests, to "imagine a communication theory that makes no reference to the individual mind" (p. 391). A consideration of the author or the sender would not be necessary to this discourse at all. Once the text is out there, the author is irrelevant. At best, she is just another reader. You will come to realize that your understanding of this text is not the result of an idea traveling from my mind to your mind. It is the result of a unique interaction which you are having with this text that you hold before your eyes. Just on the basis of this short self-reflection of what you, the reader, are doing at this very moment, you realize that *it is possible* to conceive of a discourse of communication that does not rely on the notion of the matching of ideas.

A Semiotic Discourse of Communication

The relationship between a text and a reader, as opposed to the relationship between a sender and a receiver, is the central theme that runs throughout the theoretical works of semiotician Umberto Eco, who is perhaps the most well-known European cultural and literary theorist of the twentieth century (Radford, 2003). Eco attempts to articulate an understanding of the situation in which you find yourself at this very moment: How it is you are able to make sense of this book that you are holding in your hands. Consider the following questions:

- What does this text mean? In itself? To you? To some other reader?
- What are the codes that enable your understanding of these words?
- What competence are you relying on to make sense of this text?
- How is misinterpretation possible? Or over-interpretation?
- How does this text connect with other texts?
- Does the meaning of this text reside in these words or as part of a network of knowledge?
- What is the nature of this network?
- Where does interpretation start? More importantly, where does it stop?
- What are the limits to interpretation?

135

Questions such as these form the heart of Umberto Eco's work in the academic field known as *semiotics*. The word "semiotics" comes from the Greek root *seme*, as in *semiotikos*, an interpreter of signs in which a sign is *"everything* that, on the grounds of a previously established social convention, can be taken as standing for something else" (Eco, 1976, p. 16). The term "semeiotics" originally referred to the branch of medical science relating to the interpretation of symptoms (Simpson & Weiner, 1989, Volume XIV, p. 959). Thus, red spots "stand for" the measles, or swollen neck glands "stand for" the mumps. In its modern usage, semiotics is defined as "the science of communication studies through the interpretation of signs and symbols as they operate in various fields, esp. language" (Simpson & Weiner, 1989, Volume XIV, p. 959).

The two key terms in both of these definitions are "sign" and "interpretation." The physician considers the headache and sweaty palms as signs indicating an underlying medical condition. She reads, or interprets, the signs to arrive at a diagnosis and treatment. For semiotics, anything in a culture can be considered as a sign: a text, an image, a building, the design of a car, a hairstyle. These signs are read and a meaning imputed to them. Interpretation allows us to make sense of the objects we encounter.

The words you are reading now are signs. The presence of the words in themselves is not as important, or as interesting, as the "something else" for which they stand; the content they convey. Someone versed in the transmission regime of communication might be tempted to ask: "What is the idea that these words encode?" Orwell's O'Brien would immediately put the pain dial up to eighty at such a response! As a semiotician, Umberto Eco asks the following questions: How are *you* able to arrive at this content? How are *you* able to interpret these signs and make sense of them? Like the doctor looking at the red spots on the patient's body trying to interpret her sickness, so you too must look at these words and interpret meaning from them. This process has nothing to do with me, the author. The problem to be addressed is the process though which *you* are able to do this.

To answer the problem of communication in these terms, it is necessary to address the reader of the text rather than the ideas of the writer. So, who are you? Where has this text landed and who has picked it up? Are you an undergraduate student with a course assignment? A graduate student coming to grips with communication theory for the first time? A communication major exploring a new corner of her field? These questions are important because each reader brings something different to this text: Different backgrounds, education, exposure to European theories of communication, motives, motivation, and so on. Since this book is being written for a wide audience, and for the greatest number of readers possible, these inevitable differences in background, culture, and knowledge will lead to a number of different "readings" of this book even though the actual words and sentences remain the same for all readers. As Eco (1992) describes, this variety is the very nature of the reading experience:

> When a text is produced not for a single addressee but for a community of readers-the author knows that he or she will be interpreted not according to his or her intentions but according to a complex strategy of interactions which also involve the readers, along with their competence in language as a social treasury. (p. 67)

The important concept here is that of "social treasury":

> I mean by social treasury not only a given language as a set of grammatical rules, but also the whole encyclopedia that the performances of that language have implemented, namely the cultural conventions that that language has produced and the very history of the previous interpretations of many texts, comprehending the text that the reader is in the course of reading. (Eco, 1992, pp. 67-68)

There is a textual journey you have taken in order to reach the point at which you hold this book in your hands. You are not reading this book at random, but rather in conjunction with other texts that you have read or with which you are familiar. It may be something as mundane as a reading assignment on a syllabus for a college class. Indeed, Eco suggests that it is not *you*, the reader, who achieves comprehension, but rather the history of previous interpretations of many other texts that you have read. Your interpretation of this text falls within a system of knowledge comprised of:

- your knowledge of language as a vocabulary and set of grammatical rules,

- an encyclopedia of cultural knowledge and conventions, and

- your history of previous interpretations of other texts, some of which may be related to semiotics, while many others will not.

It is within the framework of this system, which Eco refers to as the reader's *encyclopedia*, that your understanding of this text takes place. Thus, although I may intend to convey certain themes and ideas to you, in the last analysis I have no real control as to how these words will come to be read and used. The thoughts, feelings, and ideas I may have had when I wrote these words are irrelevant to this moment you are reading them. Eco has noted "the text is there, and produces its own effects" (1983, p. 7). There is no need to contemplate the ideas of the author, since all you can see is the text.

Like Eco, Michel Foucault (1988) notes of his own writings that their effects "might land in unexpected places and form shapes that I had never thought of" (pp. 333-334). What this text means, the content it attempts to convey, is not simply contained in these words nor in the intentions of its author. As Eco points out, "the text's intention is not displayed by the textual surface . . . One has to decide to 'see' it. It is possible to speak of the text's intention only as a result of a conjunction on the part of the reader" (1992, p. 64). So we have the text. We have you, the reader. In order for you to understand the text, in order to figure out and understand the intentions that lie behind these words, you must make conjectures, hypotheses, and educated guesses. It is the interaction of your conjectures and this text that produces the meaning you derive. Richard Rorty (1992) captures this sentiment nicely when he suggests that: "reading texts is a matter of reading them in the light of other texts, people, obsessions, bits of information, or what have you, and then seeing what happens" (p. 105). How a text combines with a reader's personal and cultural encyclopedia of knowledge forms the heart of Eco's semiotic problematic.

One of the products of reading texts such as this one is the creation of the Model Reader (Eco always capitalizes the term "Model Reader"). There is an important distinction between a Model Reader and an empirical reader. The empirical reader is you, the person next to you on the bus, anyone, when you read a text. Empirical readers can read in many ways, and there is no law that tells them how to read because they often use a text for their own reasons, such as escape, entertainment, or killing time on the bus commute. It is impossible to predict with any certainty what the encyclopedia of any empirical reader will be like, how this text will fit within that encyclopedia, the uses the encyclopedia will make of this text, and the meanings it will take from it. One of the duties of the text is to provide you with the rules by which it should be read. You need to recognize and agree to the rules of the particular game that is being played. As a Model Reader, you will agree to abide by these rules in order for you to derive a coherent understanding. For example, consider the problem posed by the wolf in "Little Red Riding

Hood." We know as empirical readers with a particular world knowledge that wolves do not speak. However, as Model Readers we have to agree to live in a world where wolves do speak in order for the tale to make sense. As Model Readers, we must agree to abide by the rules of the fairy tale, where animals speak and grandmothers can be swallowed whole and alive by wolves. As Eco (1992) points out, "every act of reading is a difficult transaction between the competence of the reader (the reader's world knowledge) and the kind of competence that a given text postulates in order to be read in an economic way" (1992, p. 68).

This "difficult transaction" between a text and its reader was explicitly recognized by both Michel Foucault and Ludwig Wittgenstein. In his foreword to *The Order of Things*, Foucault (1973) writes: "This foreword should perhaps be headed 'Directions for Use.' Not because I feel that the reader cannot be trusted-he is, of course, free to make what he will of the book he has been kind enough to read. What right have I, then, to suggest that it should be used in one way rather than another?" (p. ix). Yet Foucault felt compelled to elaborate on how this most difficult book should be read because he sensed, in imagining the encyclopedias of its potential readers, many ways in which his text might be misread. Foucault (1973) writes of his book: "When I was writing it there were too many things that were not clear to me: some of these seemed too obvious, others too obscure. So I said to myself: this is how my ideal reader would have approached my book, if my intentions had been clearer and my project more ready to take form" (p. ix).

Wittgenstein wrote his first major work, the *Tractatus* (Kolak, 1998), with the sense that perhaps the majority of its readers would not have the encyclopedia necessary to understand his work and that the number of Model Readers would be small. In his preface, Wittgenstein wrote that: "This book will perhaps be understood only by those who have themselves already thought the thoughts which are expressed in it - or similar thoughts" (Kolak, 1998, p. xxxi). He continues: "Its purpose would be achieved if there were one person who read it with understanding and to whom it gave pleasure" (p. xxxi). This one person who could read the *Tractatus* with understanding and pleasure would be Wittgenstein's "Model Reader"; that reader who is able to recognize and observe the rules of the game laid out by the text, and who is eager and able to play such a game. It is interesting to contemplate the notion that you can understand a text only if you have had thoughts similar to the ones motivating the author. Does this mean that if you have not had these thoughts, the text will be incomprehensible? Well, try to read Wittgenstein's *Tractatus* or Foucault's *Order of Things* and you will see my point! The words do not appear unfamiliar, or the grammar. Both follow the rules of the English language. It is the rules by which the text is to be read that both Foucault and Wittgenstein struggle to articulate and about which they express reservations.

Eco, Foucault, and Wittgenstein are three authors who let go of their texts once they have been written. They understand fully that once their texts enter the public realm, the meaning of that text is no longer theirs to dictate or control. Communication takes place between the reader and the text, not between the author and the reader. What the author thinks is of no consequence and is quite irrelevant to the understandings derived by the reader. We have a discourse of communication that does not require the matching of ideas between minds.

If you are able to accept and understand these ideas, you have made the first step in transcending a transmission regime of discourse. Like my students, you may understand these concepts now, but as soon as you put the book down and go about your daily life, the reality of the transmission view soon snaps back into place again. But there may have been a moment, a few seconds perhaps, when Eco's point of view made sense, where communication really didn't require a sender and didn't consist of ideas moving from one brain to another. You will have reached a place similar to that of Winston early in his tortuous ordeal with O'Brien:

> "Just now I held up the fingers of my hand to you. You saw five fingers. Do you remember that?"
> "Yes."
> O'Brien held up the fingers of his left hand, with thumb concealed.
> "There are five fingers there. Do you see five fingers?"
> "Yes."
> And he did see them, for a fleeting instant, before the scenery of his mind changed. He saw five fingers, and there was no deformity. Then everything was normal again, and the old fear, the hatred, and the bewilderment came crowding back again. But there had been a moment-he did not know how long, thirty seconds, perhaps-of luminous certainty, when each new suggestion of O'Brien's had filled up a patch of emptiness and became absolute truth, and when two and two could have been three as easily as five, if that were what was needed. It had faded out before O'Brien had dropped his hand; but though he could not recapture it, he could remember it, as one remembers a vivid experience at some remote period of one's life when one was in effect a different person.

"You see now," said O'Brien, "that it is at any rate possible."

"Yes," said Winston. (Orwell, 1949/1984, p. 213)

Signs and Indications

For our next session deep in the bowels of Orwell's Ministry of Love, I want to discuss with you another discourse of communication that does not make reference to the individual mind: the philosophy of Czech philosopher Edmund Husserl (1859-1938) as described in the *Logical Investigations* (Husserl, 1900/1970). In this work, Husserl was not concerned with language and meaning for their own sake. His major objective was to develop and articulate a refutation of psychologism, the view that the laws of logic are descriptions of regularities in the way we think. In many important respects, Husserl's refutation of psychologism complements our objective here; to challenge the view that communication is a reflection of our individual thoughts and mental states. In his refutation of psychologism, Husserl developed a way of speaking about communication that does not rely on the premise that meaning is dependent upon ideas in the mind or that communication has anything to do with the transmission of ideas from one place to another. Introducing Husserl's account is intended to give us more linguistic resources with which to imagine a communication theory that makes no reference to the individual mind.

Central to understanding Husserl's theory of meaning is his distinction between "signs" and "expressions." Husserl's description of signs will look very familiar to us within the regime of communication. It outlines a view of communication very similar to John Locke's. But in his explication of the nature of "expressions," Husserl will offer a theory of meaning that goes beyond a Lockean view of meaning. It is to Husserl's account of "expressions," then, that we will turn in order to transcend our familiar Lockean view, just as Husserl does. But first we must understand what Husserl means by "signs" and how it is similar to the Lockean view.

There is nothing mysterious or difficult about Husserl's use of the term "sign." A sign is something that stands for something else such as smoke being a sign of fire. Husserl offers the examples of the brand being the sign of a slave and the flag being the sign of a nation. These marks help us to recognize the objects to which they are attached. The sign is said to *indicate* or point to the presence of something else.

But indication goes further than simply being a mark for something else. For example, Martian canals, as signs, might indicate the existence of intelligent beings on Mars. Fossil vertebrae, as signs, might indicate the existence of prediluvian animals. These are not self-evident connections that are inherent in the sign and the thing referred to. Such connections have to be created by a person who reasons that such a connection is logical or appropriate. Husserl's examples of the Martian canals and the fossil vertebrae reveal to him that indication is a property of the person, not the sign and the referent. As Husserl (1900/1970) points out: "A thing is only properly an indication if and where it in fact serves to indicate something to some thinking being" (p. 270). Therefore, indication requires a preexisting state of knowledge within the person to complete the relationship between the sign and thing the sign stands for. As Husserl (1900/1970) describes, "certain objects or states of affairs *of whose reality someone has actual knowledge* indicate to him *the reality of certain other objects or states of affairs*" (p. 270). Husserl refers to this as a "descriptive unity" (p. 270); indication is an *act of judgment* in which indicating and indicated states of affairs become constituted by the thinker. Such subjective acts of inference are made according to the logic of the syllogism: "Certain things *may* or *must* exist, *since* other things have been given" (Husserl, 1900/1970, p. 270). However, this does not mean to say that what one infers is real or true:

> When one says that the state of affairs *A* indicates the state of affairs *B*, that the existence of the one points to that of the other, one may confidently be expecting to find *B* true, but one's mode of speech implies no objectively necessary conditions between *A* and *B*, nothing into which one could have insight. (Husserl, 1900/1970, p. 272)

Such acts of inference are, at best, hypotheses. Therefore, indication is always a relationship of probability, or of contingency. The existence of one thing furnishes the ground of probability for the existence of another thing. The presence of volcanic phenomena may or may not indicate that the earth's interior is molten. When I observe an emotional expression on the face of my daughter, I am free to infer the presence of a particular emotional state that may have provoked it. But my inference about her internal state is always my hypothesis. I cannot know directly what she is feeling. There is no feeling or idea that is transmitted to me by her expression. There is only the feeling I infer by taking her expression to be a sign of some other state of affairs, namely her emotional state.

Husserl's (1900/1970) notion of communication is built upon this notion of indication and has many similarities to Locke's account:

The articulate sound-complex, the written sign etc., first becomes a spoken word or a communicative bit of speech, when a speaker produces it with the intention of "expressing himself about something" through its means; he must endow it with a sense in certain acts of mind, a sense he desires to share with his auditors. (pp. 276-277)

Husserl (1900/1970) continues:

Such sharing becomes a possibility if the auditor also understands the speaker's intention. He does this inasmuch as he takes the speaker to be a person, who is not merely uttering sounds but *speaking to him*. (p. 277)

Therefore,

What first makes mental commerce possible, and turns connected speech into discourse, lies in the correlation among corresponding physical and mental experiences of communicating persons which is effected by the physical side of speech. (p. 277)

This description of communication as the correlation of corresponding mental experiences (what the listener has in her mind corresponds to what the speaker has in his mind) leads Husserl to the following important conclusion: "All expressions in *communicative* speech function as *indications*. They serve the hearer as signs of the 'thoughts' of the speaker" (Husserl, 1900/1970, p. 277). Husserl refers to this concept as the "intimating function" of verbal expressions. To understand an intimation is not to have conceptual knowledge of it. It simply means that "the hearer *intuitively* takes the speaker to be a person who is expressing this or that" (p. 277). The hearer perceives him as such.

At the level of indication, communication with a person is little different from communicating with your cat. Both the person and the cat perform actions. The person may utter sounds, give facial expressions, and make gestures. The cat may meow and rub against your legs. All of these actions can be taken as signs to someone who is perceiving them. The leap to seeing these actions as signs of something deeper is always taken by the perceiver. And these leaps can be quite large. For example, my students are very eager to tell me about their cat's personality.

"How do you know they have a personality?" I ask.

"Because he likes to snuggle on my lap," they say. Or, "He always wakes me up by licking my face in the morning."
"So what does this tell you about the personality of your cat?" I ask.
"It tells me he's friendly. It tells me that he loves me. It tells me he is a happy cat," they say.

Students also tell me how their cats "communicate" their emotions, hunger, and intentions. In Husserl's terms, this is all a quite accurate use of the term "communication." The expressions of the animals are performing an intimating function. It is the perceiver that takes the animal's acts as signs of something else. Whether the cat is really communicating some inner mental content is anyone's guess. The same is the case for communicating with other people. As Husserl (1900/1970) explains:

> The hearer perceives the speaker as manifesting certain inner experiences, and to that extent he also perceives these experiences themselves: he does not, however, himself experience them, he has not an "inner" but an "outer" percept of them. (p. 278)

This outer percept is an inference. Again, this is consistent with the Locke model. Expressions in communication operate indicatively. So, the facial expression of the cat is not indicative of any real "mood" or "personality" of the cat. The connection between the expression and the "mood" is created by the perceiver drawing upon a knowledge of how things are related to each other. The person learned that "motor-boat purring" stands for "feeling happy." Similarly, when we see a person smile, we associate that perception with "feeling happy" and attribute this mental state to the person. The same is the case when the person produces an utterance such as "I feel happy." But the utterance "I feel happy" does not stand for such a state in any real sense. It is entirely possible that the person is telling a lie, for instance. Even though they tell you that they feel happy, they may actually be feeling sad or angry. The person may smile at you even though they feel quite depressed. We can only infer that since the person has told you they feel happy or that they smiled at us, then these signs *probably* indicate an underlying emotional state of happiness. But this is an association made by the perceiver and not the sender. By itself, the facial expression, either by a person or by your cat, means nothing:

> It is not to the point that another person may interpret our involuntary manifestations, e.g., our "expressive movement," and that he may thereby become deeply acquainted with our inner

144

thoughts and emotions. They "mean" something to him insofar as he interprets them, but even for him they are without meaning in the special sense in which verbal signs have meaning: they only mean in the sense of indicating. (Husserl, 1900/1970, p. 275)

Husserl's conclusion is clear: "To mean *is not a particular way of being a sign in the sense of indicating something*" (p. 269). There is something else to meaning that cannot be accounted for by the relationship of a sign and the thing it stands for. From this starting point, Husserl will be able to develop a theory of meaning that does not rely on the premise that signs (utterances, marks on paper) gain their meaning from the mental states they indicate. The existence of a mental state behind the words is simply not necessary.

Husserl is able to support this claim quite vividly by giving an example in which a sign can have meaning without standing for a mental state. Husserl describes a situation with which we are all very familiar. Consider those times when you sit in quiet reflection. You are sitting in your favorite chair. You are relaxed. The television is turned off. You are enjoying a glass of wine while you read this book in splendid isolation and quiet. Your thoughts begin to roam: What do I need to accomplish tomorrow? How could I have handled that meeting better today? What is my girlfriend going to think of my new haircut? You are engaging in soliloquy, a dialogue with yourself. You are thinking using verbal expressions. You work through your thoughts using language. All of these expressions within soliloquy have meanings. They also have the same meanings that would arise if I were to express these thoughts in a dialogue with another person. The ability for you to soliloquize makes it clear that the presence of a listener is not necessary in order for your expressions to have meaning. As Husserl (1900/1970) points out, "when we live in the understanding of a word, it expresses something and the same thing, whether we address it to anyone or not" (p. 278-279).

This demonstrates for Husserl that an expression's meaning does not need to coincide with any particular feat of intimation, which is the basis of communication. If this were so, then we would have to say that even in mental soliloquy, one uses expressions to intimate something to oneself. But what are the things indicated in the expressions of a private soliloquy? My mental states? My ideas? But why would I need to produce an expression that would *stand for* or indicate my ideas when I am already in possession of those ideas? What would be the point of (a) having an idea, (b) encoding it into an expression, (c) decoding that expression (i.e., inferring what the expression stands for), and (d) having an idea, when I am the one who had the original idea? Why do I need a sign of my own experiences, when I have, even better, the experiences themselves?

In soliloquy, words function as signs here as they do everywhere else. They can be still said to point to something. But they do *not point to mental states*:

> In the genuine sense of communication, there is no speech in such cases, nor does one tell onself anything: one merely conceives of oneself as speaking and communicating. In a monologue, words can perform no function of indicating the existence of mental acts, since such indication would be quite purposeless. For the acts in question are themselves experienced by us at that very moment. (Husserl, 1900/1970, p. 280)

As Husserl so vividly demonstrates, indication is not necessary for meaning. "*Expressions* function meaningfully even in *isolated mental life, where they no longer serve to indicate anything*" (p. 269). There is no separation of thought and sign. There is no need to perceive the sign and then work back to the mental state it points to. The two are joined in a fundamental unity and we experience them as a unity. The transmission regime of communication asks us to imagine a consciousness that is prior to experience: that stands against the world, receives sensations, turns them into perceptual objects, and then bases an interpretation on them. For Husserl, there is no such separation. Indeed, his example of the soliloquy shows there is no need for such a separation. If *A* summons *B* into consciousness, we are not merely simultaneously or successively conscious of both *A* and *B*, but we usually *feel* their connection forcing itself upon us. For example, look at this sign:

DOG

Try to see this sign as marks on paper, an arrangement of black lines on a white background, without seeing it as the word "dog." It is almost impossible to separate the sign DOG (the physical marks on this page) and the word "dog" which comes complete with the meanings this word has for you. You do not see the sign DOG and then, in some separate process, search your mind for the appropriate object the word stands for, bring that object into consciousness, and bring the sign and the word together. You see the sign DOG and the word "dog" together as a fundamental unity. We are, as Husserl (1900/1970) puts it, "differently minded" (p. 303) in respect of it: "it no longer seems a mere sensuous mark on paper, the physical phenomenon counts as an *understood* sign" (p. 303). Husserl calls this "living understandingly"-"we perform no act of presentation or judgment directed upon the sign as a sensible object, but another act, quite different in kind" (p. 303). It is the nature of this other act, "quite different in kind," that we now turn.

Expressions and Communication

Husserl is proposing a way of talking about communication in which meaning is something quite independent of any empirical process, whether that process be the manner in which an expression is expressed as a physical sign or by the physical processes inherent in a living brain. Husserl will claim that meaning is *not* dependent on your thoughts or mental imagery. For example, consider the following expression:

My cat is beautiful.

At one level, "My cat is beautiful" is a sign. It consists of marks on paper. I can vary the way "My cat is beautiful" is presented on this page by using different sizes and fonts, like so:

My cat is beautiful.

My cat is beautiful.

My cat is beautiful.

My cat is beautiful.

MY CAT IS BEAUTIFUL.

The point Husserl is making is that no matter how I change the size or the font, the meaning of "My cat is beautiful" remains the same. The same is the case for spoken speech. I can say "My cat is beautiful" quickly, slowly, with

147

a stutter, at a high pitch or a low pitch, and the meaning of the expression will remain the same. When I write "My cat is beautiful," I may have a particular psychological attitude. Maybe I am happy, sad, excited, angry, or indifferent. Again, my state of mind will not change the meaning of "My cat is beautiful." Even if you infer that my emotional state is related to my vocal expression, such that the high volume and pitch of my voice indicates anger, still the meaning of "My cat is beautiful" remains the same.

The process of making sense of "My cat is beautiful" has its own conditions and requirements apart from the empirical nature of its presentation. Husserl's approach to communication goes beyond the physical nature of the message in order to study the structures of sense-making and meaning structures in their own right. To do this, Husserl uses a method called "bracketing" in which "all assumptions about nature and empirical phenomena, all being, in brief all reality, must be placed in parenthesis, must be set aside as if it were an irrelevant function in experience" (Pilotta & Mickunas, 1990, p. 11). This method essentially means bracketing all the assumptions of a Lockean view of communication since none of the empirical and physical manifestations of communication phenomenon are of concern. This includes the physical form of the message and its presentation, the empirical mental states of the person sending the message and the empirical mental states of the person receiving the message.

The Lockean view assumes that something concrete and real "happens" in the mind of the sender which, through the transmission of a message, causes something concrete and real to "happen" in the mind of the receiver. When my students tell me that their ideas are "encoded" in language and that a receiver "decodes" their message, they are telling me that empirically real processes of encoding and decoding actually happen somewhere in their respective brains. When they "interpret" a message, or retrieve an image from their memory, something physical is going on. It is only when I attempt to have them describe the nature of these real processes that they fall into trouble. In Husserl's approach to communication, all of these questions are moot because they are bracketed. We simply do not assume that the possibility of communication is related to an empirical process. We do not seek an explanation in terms of "something that happens" in the mind or brain. We seek to understand communication in terms of structures of meaning and sense-making that have no physical counterpart. When presented with:

My cat is beautiful.

we do not seek to understand this statement in terms of its physical characteristics (its size, font, position on the page) or the brain processes that occurred when I wrote this, or the brain processes that occurred in your head when you read this. We know that any of these things can be altered and varied, yet the meaning of "My cat is beautiful" will remain the same. What Husserl seeks to describe is: What is it about "My cat is beautiful" that remains the same even when its physical concomitants change and vary? What is the essence of this expression? Clearly it is something different from its physical manifestation.

The sentence "My cat is beautiful," as it appears before you on this page, is a physical instantiation (a token) of something that is not physical (a type). Consider the word "CAR." I would assume that every reader of this book understands the meaning of "CAR." However, if I were to ask you to show me "CAR," you would not be able to do so. You could point to your Honda Accord in the parking lot and say "look, that is a car." I would look and certainly agree with you. I could also point to the Ford Taurus or the Toyota Camry, or one those new Mini-Coopers, and say "look, those are cars also, but they look quite different from the car you pointed out." For a start, they have different body shapes. They are all painted different colors. There are an infinite number of empirical differences between all the cars in the parking lot. There are an infinite number of empirical differences between the Honda you pointed out and any other "car" you or I would care to point to, whether it be on the street where I live, or in the township of Morris, the state of New Jersey, the Eastern Seaboard of the United States, or in any country in the world. From this infinite empirical variation, what is it that enables you to identify any of these objects as "cars" and, more particularly, enables you to identify the Honda as a "car"?

It soon becomes apparent that one cannot experience "CAR" at all. All we can do is experience examples of the category. Your Honda is an example of a car, so is that Mini-Cooper. These particular examples are empirical tokens of a particular eidetic type-"CAR." Husserl would not be interested in any particular physical car. He is interested in the nature and the structure of the "CAR" by which you are able to perceive, identify, and communicate about the Honda in the parking lot. This "CAR" is not physical. It is not a memory, or a mental state, or a stored experience, or a neural algorithm that fires in your brain. It is meaning pure unto itself that operates beyond the bounds of empirical reality.

Husserl's view is not skeptical, however. It does not deny the existence of reality, brains, or mental processes. Bracketing is intended to direct our attention away from our naturalistic impulses. It attempts to get us away from questions such as: How does that happen? How does the brain make

149

that happen? Husserl attempts to put out of play the naturalistic assumption to enable the investigation of the experiential dimension-the dimension of the "CAR." Bracketing reveals an absolute domain that is not dependent on any physical manifestation, since all these are contingent and constantly changing. In the midst of all this empirical variation and change, our experience of "CAR" is essential.

Consider the perceptual process of looking at this book. Hold it up. Look at it. You can move it around and view it from different sides and angles. Despite these changes in distance and perspective, the "book" before you remains constant. It doesn't become a different object just because it changes shape and size. The "book" itself is totally distinct from the perceptual process. Husserl would say that the "book" is *transcendent*. It exists apart from and outside of your perceptual process.

Neither can we say that the book "causes" your perceptual process. When you look at the front cover of this book, the unseen back cover cannot "cause" you to turn the book over in order to view it. As Pilotta and Mickunas (1990) point out:

> Without the structure of identical and continuous "transcendent" object and the variation of perceptual activities, no experience would be possible. At this level something must remain identical and continuous to which the various perceptual acts are correlated; otherwise with each act the object would be different and no continuity between the acts would be given. (p. 13)

All acts of perception assume a continuity. You see this book. You touch it, feel it, walk around it, throw it on the floor, put it on the bookshelf. Throughout all of these activities, the "book" remains the same. Also, this book itself is always changing. It may look new and shiny today and have that new book smell. Tomorrow it may have creases in the spine as it is bent to turn the pages. Pages become dog-eared, you scribble notes in the margins, you squish it on a photocopier to make copies of page 72 for your class. Over time the pages will turn yellow and the glue in the spine will crumble. And yet, despite these changes, it will remain the same "book." Perceptually, the empirical book changes all the time. You can never see it the same way twice. It has changed and you have changed. What is constant about the book is not something that is given in perception. There must be another level of experience that is not perceptual, but essential. There must be an "essence."

Husserl does not ask whether or not these essences "exist" in the ontological sense. Remember, Husserl brackets all claims to empirical reality. It is enough to know that such essences are necessary. Experience is involved with essential insights even when such insights remain mere possibilities and may never have a perceptual correlate. For example, consider the task of teaching arithmetic to a child. There are many ways to do this. You might use blocks, fingers, or diagrams. What is important is not the perceptual objects used, but the learning of essential arithmetic *insights* that are not themselves perceptual. The essential insight is not derived from the various objects used to exemplify arithmetic relations. The real objects are bracketed, leaving the insight that is essential. It is not dependent on the objects: "the facts are contingent, the experiential insight into their contingency is essential" (Pilotta & Mickunas, 1990, p. 16).

Experience, Essence, and Communication

The insight into essence in experience is one of the conditions for communication. When we communicate, we often do not have the perceptual objects before us. Earlier, I told you that "My cat is beautiful." I even put this sentence in a number of different fonts and sizes. Even though you cannot see my cat, or even know if I have one or not, you are still able to understand my expression. Even if my cat were present, or if I had a photograph of my cat before us in the book, both you and I could never see the same object or see it from exactly the same perspective. Your perception of the object and mine are different. Our perceptions are distinct sensations. Yet, in communication, we can both agree that we see the same cat. What allows communication to happen is the having of an insight into the essence of what a cat is as a type.

We might be tempted to say that what we are doing is retrieving a memory of a prior experience of a cat and then making a comparison. Even if this were the case, the essential insight into "CAT" is still necessary in order to know what memories to compare with the present perception. After all, if a person associates a present perceptual experience with a previous experience from memory, those two experiences would not be alike. And, if two people are communicating about the same cat, the memories they bring to make sense of the object would also be different. So how can they be talking about the same thing? The invocation of previous experience to explain a current experience does not clarify the current experience. It simply adds more experiences that need to be explained. It's like asking me to explain what I mean by the words "My cat is beautiful." Well, I could say "My cat has a shiny coat" or "My cat has a cute face." All I am doing is providing more words on top of my previous words.

The essence, then, is not intrinsic to the experiencing subject. It is not something inside me that I bring to bear on a current experience. It is not a memory or something I have stored in my mind. Rather, it is an object of experience. It is not bound by space and time and is a fundamental requirement of communication.

Although the means of communication (sounds, marks on paper, etc.) are temporal, the structure of the communicative process, and the objects about which this process is engaged, is not temporal. It is accessible to anyone at any time. When you read a theoretical treatise from the past, such as when you read the text of this book, these marks on this paper, you have no empirical evidence of any author. You have never met me. For all you know, I may be long dead. You cannot check the way I received the empirical impressions that created these words. You do not know the surroundings that caused such impressions.

Yet, here you are, reading these pages with enjoyment and understanding. You know what is being communicated, even though you do not know me or when and how these words were written. You can never be in "my position" to know where these words came from. But as you know by now, none of these considerations is important to your experience of this text. The empirical circumstances of its production are totally contingent.

All of this goes against the dominant Lockean view of communication. The *causal* relationship between the means of transmitting the message and the person being affected by such means does *not* constitute the communication process. The talk of larynxes causing molecules to vibrate, hitting your ear, and sending signals to the brain, etc., is not what is essential to communication. My handwriting style or my choice of font does not constitute the rules of grammar. Rather, the rules of grammar are exemplified in my writing, my speaking, and other forms of expression. The empirical manifestations of communication (words, molecules, sounds, brains) do not present a complete view of communication. Husserl raises our awareness that communication is concerned with experiential essences, of experiential insights, which are not empirical. When we communicate about a spatial object, we are involved in the essential aspects given in experience. When we communicate about my cat being beautiful, we are involved with the essential insights concerning what a "CAT" is and what "BEAUTIFUL" means. These are not definitions, nor memories of past experiences, but a direct experience of an essential insight. The experience of essences is not reducible to empirical phenomena. These are not things you can find or see.

When I write these words about Husserl and communication, I do not require that you, the reader, have had the same perceptual experiences or similar subjective internal mental states to understand what I am saying. Of course you understand. You understand that what you see before you are words and sentences. You understand that what you see before you is text. You also recognize that what you see are meaningful expressions. You do not take meaning *out* of these words, like the conduit metaphor suggest. You do not take something out that I have somehow put in. The meaning is experienced as a fundamental unity. When I read Husserl's (1900/1970) *Logical Investigations*, I do not need to know Husserl in order to understand the expressions he has left behind in his text. To reiterate Eco's (1983) words at the beginning of this chapter, "the author should die once he has finished writing. So as not to trouble the path of the text" (p. 7). Husserl died in 1938, yet his text remains and his expressions continue to have meaning. His death does not diminish the meaning of his text in any way. Indeed, his death liberates the text from our belief that somehow Husserl has the correct interpretation, if only we could discover it. We no longer need to regard the *Logical Investigations* as a message *from* Husserl. Instead, Husserl has provided us with a very different way of talking about communication that does not make reference to individual minds or mechanisms of transmission. In the following chapter, I will offer two further discourses that also speak of communication in this manner.

Eight
A Hermeneutic Discourse of Communication:
The Genuine Conversation

We say that we "conduct" a conversation, but the more genuine a conversation is, the less its conduct lies within the will of either partner. Thus a genuine conversation is never the one that we wanted to conduct. (Hans-Georg Gadamer)

In chapter seven, I introduced Eco's semiotics and Husserl's *Logical Investigations* as potential entry points to different and competing ways of speaking about communication. The term "communication" is still used in these new regimes, but the *way it is used* is quite different. As a consequence, the worlds in which communication resides will be much different from the world of the transmission regime of communication. Not only will the world be different, *we* will be different. In Orwell's (1949) *1984*, O'Brien succeeded in changing Winston by subverting his language of an autonomous self and creating a conversation in which that language did not and could not make sense. I will attempt to do the same in this chapter. No longer will the term "communication" appear alongside terms such as "sender," "receiver," "encode," "decode," and "transmission." Instead I will present "communication" in the context of a much different constellation of terms such as "interpretation," "understanding," and "conversation." "Communication" will no longer refer to the transmission of ideas from one mind to another, but to the mutual creation of meaning in the flow of a living genuine conversation. The name of this regime is hermeneutics.

The etymology of the term "hermeneutics" has a relationship to Hermes, the messenger god of the Greeks. In order to deliver the messages of the gods, Hermes had to be conversant in their language as well as the language of the mortals for whom the messages were intended. There were two parts to Hermes's task:

- He had to understand and translate for himself what the gods wanted to convey to the world; and

- He had to translate and articulate this message to the mortals.

There is clearly a model of communication here that looks familiar to us in the transmission regime. Hermes is carrying a message from the gods (the senders) to the mortals (the receivers). But the hermeneutic problem is *not* concerned with what happens in the *minds* of the gods or the *minds* of the mortals. Instead it seeks to address *the role of Hermes* and his ability to understand a discourse from one domain (the gods) and articulate that understanding within a very different domain (that of the mortals). Hermes represents the *labor* and the *effort* required to read and understand texts produced in one place and time and to articulate their meanings in a different place and time.

Hermeneutics received its first systematic formulation in the proper interpretation of biblical and sacred texts (Deetz, 1977). The problem facing the biblical scholar is essentially the same as Hermes's problem communicating messages between the gods and the mortals. How can a biblical scholar accurately and correctly interpret the message of God as it is expressed through the Bible and then express this meaning in terms that a language community, located in a particular space and time, can understand? While the message of God is fixed and universal, the social and historical contexts of readers vary greatly. Different communities, and even different readers within those communities, can interpret the word of God in different ways depending on their encyclopedias. The hermeneutic was intended to address this problem and render the true meaning of the biblical text, written in one time and place, intelligible to the people of a different time and place. As Paul Ricoeur (1974) points out, "the very work of interpretation reveals a profound intention, that of overcoming distance and cultural differences and of matching the reader to a text which has become foreign" (p. 4). Ricouer's talk of "overcoming distance" and "matching the reader to a text" is not describing the transmission of meaning from one time or place to another, as if that meaning could travel intact. Nothing "moves" in hermeneutics. The focus is on the effort brought to bear by the reader in her attempt to render intelligible a text that was previously considered to be alien and strange.

According to David Linge (1976), hermeneutics is concerned with all those situations in which we encounter meanings that are not immediately understandable. The understanding of these meanings requires interpretive effort. You should find this situation very familiar. You may be experiencing the feeling of "interpretive effort" right now in trying to understand what I am saying about hermeneutics, especially if this is a new domain of knowledge for you. Consider also the following situations:

- You are looking at an abstract painting in the Museum of Modern Art.
- You are reading a poem or a work of literature.
- You are reading Edmund Husserl's (1900/1970) *Logical Investigations* for the first time.
- You are listening to a lecture on hermeneutics being given by your communication professor.

In each of these situations you are being presented with something that is new, alien, and potentially difficult to understand. What these texts mean is not at all obvious or self-evident. Understanding these texts requires effort on your part. As Linge (1976) points out: "in all these cases, the hermeneutical has to do with bridging the gap between the familiar world in which we stand and the strange meaning that resists assimilation into the horizons of our world" (p. xii). Your understanding of these texts requires that you take a text produced in one time and place and contextualize it with respect to a personal encyclopedia, or "social treasury," to use Eco's term, produced in a different time and place.

I think of myself writing the text of the previous chapter on Edmund Husserl's *Logical Investigations* and I can completely identify with Hermes's situation. First I must read Husserl's text and, through significant interpretive effort on my part, attempt to understand the meaning of that text. I do not understand the text of the *Logical Investigations* by trying to know what Husserl knew. I am not trying to understand *him*. Rather, I think of me, in 2003, in my situation, at this point in my life and my academic maturity. How does this modern situation produce my understanding of a text written by a German and published 103 years ago in 1900? How does my past enter into this present? How does it enable me to make the alien into something familiar? And then I think of you, my reader. How are you to understand these words I have written about Husserl's text? What do you bring to this understanding? Again, you are not trying to understand *me*. And you are certainly not trying to understand Husserl. You are making sense of a text that you hold in your hand *now*. You are trying to make a text that is unfamiliar into something familiar. The resources you bring to bear to make that happen are something far beyond my ability to predict or control. In addition, they are certainly beyond the late Professor Husserl's ability to control. But that is not important. A hermeneutic discourse of communication encompasses both the alien text we strive to understand and the familiar world that we already understand. What we need to describe is the *fusion* of the text with the contemporary context in which it is being read.

By introducing a discussion of hermeneutics in this book, I am not suggesting that a hermeneutic discourse of communication is "correct" or "superior" to an understanding of communication derived from a transmission regime. The force and vitality of the hermeneutic approach lies in its opposition and challenge to the existing world views of a transmission regime of communication. Hermeneutics should not be seen as simply another method that is somehow complementary to the transmission viewpoint. It is not another tool to be employed in the communication researcher's toolbox. It is not another theory to be covered in the Introduction to Communication class. To ask what hermeneutics can say about communication is already a loaded and ultimately misleading question. By asking the question in this manner, we are implicitly buying into the assumption that communication can exist as an autonomous entity that can be objectively studied, and that a method such as hermeneutics can somehow shed further light on it. However, by asking that question, we are also implicitly adopting a transmission regime of communication that hermeneutics seeks to question.

I want this discussion of hermeneutics to create doubt in your belief in the transmission regime of communication. To discuss hermeneutics as a philosophy and method is to discuss a discursive world very different from the regime of communication so familiar to you and my students. To understand this world, you must become a Model Reader in Eco's sense. You must agree to abide by the rules of the new world this new discourse makes possible, and give up the real world understandings provided by your previous regime of communication. A Model Reader gives up her knowledge that wolves do not speak in order to read and appreciate "Little Red Riding Hood." Similarly, a Model Reader of hermeneutics must give up her "knowledge" that communication is a function of her brain and objective information processing routines.

As we prepare to leave behind the familiar terrain of our transmission discourse, the language of hermeneutics may, at first, seem different and strange. You read the terms, but you fail to see the reality to which they refer. The adoption of such a radically different world view is never an easy task because it is so difficult to part with traditional ways of seeing and explaining. It is so tempting to consider the new approach in terms of the old. As Harre, Clarke, and De Carlo (1985) make clear in their discussion of a hermeneutic psychology of human action:

> The new approaches to theory and method of enquiry in some well-established field are often made more difficult by a natural and persistent tendency to understand new ideas in terms of the old ways. It is important to realize that the approach we have chosen to call "the psychology of action". . . is not just a revision or modification of old ways of doing psychology but a radically different approach to the understanding of human behavior. It is not just an additional theory inserted into existing psychology but a thoroughgoing alternative to it. (p. viii)

In contemporary texts on hermeneutic approaches to human action and communication, the first task to be performed is a critique of the prevailing transmission regime of communication. Before the hermeneutic approach can be described, the prevailing world view has to be discounted. Before O'Brien can impress upon Winston the Party's construction of the world, he must first destroy Winston's prevailing constructions. In this spirit, Harre and Secord's (1972) hermeneutic theory of human action is presented alongside a critique of the traditional realist notion of an experimental social psychology. The same is true of the psychology of human action described in Harre, Clarke, and De Carlo (1985) and John Shotter's explicitly hermeneutic account of human selfhood (Shotter, 1975, 1984; Gauld & Shotter, 1977). This has also been the strategy employed in this book. A hermeneutic theory of communication and human behavior is always a theory in tension with and in opposition to prevailing views of the world. That is why hermeneutics is so frequently misunderstood when it is evaluated with respect to criteria appropriate to a transmission regime.

What you must attempt to do is to read the new discourse in its own terms, without feeling the need to translate back into the familiar transmission language. This is difficult to do at first, as it is difficult to learn any new language. With continued immersion in and use of the new discourse, the world it constitutes soon comes into focus, and you will wonder why you ever believed that communication involved some bizarre process of ideas moving across space from one mind to another.

A Role for Ideas and Mental States

There is a certain sense of direction to the understanding of communication within the transmission regime. Communication begins *inside* the mind of a sender and ends *inside* the mind of a receiver. The movement of a message is like a rabbit running from hole to hole; appearing from inside one hole, running across the field, and disappearing into another hole. From a transmission point of view, to understand the nature of the message, we need to understand what the rabbit is doing inside those holes. In the discourse of Wilhelm Dilthey, understanding communication has a very different sense of direction.

Wilhelm Dilthey (1833-1911) was a German philosopher who is best known for his pioneering contributions toward a new foundation for the theory and methodology of the human sciences. Not unlike John Locke, Dilthey was interested in using the concept of internal mental states as a means of understanding human behavior and achievement. He considered psychology to be a foundational discipline that would ultimately form the basis for understanding all of the other disciplines of human studies: history, literature, law, art, philosophy, music, architecture, and religion. For Dilthey (1894/1976a), all of these ways of organizing human activity originate from "the living context of the human mind and, ultimately, can only be understood through it" (p. 90).

For example, Dilthey argues that an appropriate analysis of the nature of religion will ultimately require an understanding of psychological concepts such as "will," "feeling," "dependence," and "motive." Similarly, an account of jurisprudence will ultimately require an understanding of psychological concepts such "norm" and "accountability." The purpose of Dilthey's psychology, then, is not to understand what goes on *inside* the mind, but rather how the mind objectifies itself in social activity, institutions, and products. The importance of psychology for Dilthey is not the search *inwards* into the rabbit hole of the individual mind, but *outwards* as a means to understand the *products* of the human mind: that is, in forms of social organization, culture, art, and literature.

The relationship between the human mind and forms of social organization is always a reflexive one. Not only do the mental capabilities of the mind comprise the shaping forces behind systems of social organization and their products. The social organization so produced also both enables and constrains the capabilities of the mind. Dilthey proposed that an individual both *shapes* and is *shaped by* the cultural context in which she lives. Mental life does not exist or operate in a vacuum. Mental life is always determined by a cultural context that it has also helped to create.

The claim that thoughts arise and are made possible by a context is one that may, on the surface, seem unproblematic. But it is an idea that does not square with the transmission regime, and my students often have trouble reconciling the two. For example, students often tell me that their ideas, motives, and thoughts are produced *inside* their heads. This explanation is consistent with the transmission regime which suggests that *first* a sender has an idea and *second* the idea is encoded, transmitted, and communicated. Students are quite comfortable with this two-step process. So it is clear to them where the message comes from. It is derived from their idea. But where, I ask them, does the idea come from? Why did this idea enter your thoughts in the first place? What provoked the emergence of this idea?

Clearly, the impetus for an idea cannot be another idea. All I need to ask then is "where did that idea come from" and continue into an infinite regress. The impetus must come from somewhere outside of the mind, and so we must look to the context. So, I ask the students a question such as:

"What is the relationship between ideas and communication?"

A typical student answer would be: "First I have an idea, then I communicate that idea to my friend."

Then I say: "Why did you just tell me that?"

The students have a couple of options here. They can tell me (a) that the sentence is an encoding of an idea in their head (at which point I must turn the pain dial up to ninety!), or (b) it is a response to a question that I asked them. After all, the phrase:

"First I have an idea, then I communicate that idea to a friend"

did not emerge spontaneously or randomly. It occurred as an appropriate utterance in response to my question, which itself is part of an ongoing conversation.

So then I can ask: "Why did I ask you that question about ideas and communication?" Because it is interesting? Because I am sadistic? This question is not an utterance that comes up in your everyday dinner conversation. It came up because I am a professor of communication teaching a class in communication theory in which the topic of the day is Wilhelm Dilthey's view of psychology. My utterance is not a sign of the spontaneous appearance of a thought within my mind. It is part of the context of this classroom situation, my position as communication professor, their position as students, the place we find ourselves with respect to a syllabus, and the point we have reached in a conversation. My question and the student's answer are determined in large part by this ongoing system of social organization known as the classroom.

At the same time, the context of our conversation is produced by the mental capabilities of its participants. Individual people speaking and interacting create the conversational context, which in turn structures the ways in which people speak and interact. This interaction between context and action represents a reflexive relationship in which the first element creates the second and the second element creates the first. We find ourselves both enabled and constrained by contexts of our own making. We are free to build the streets and avenues of our cities as creatively as our minds desire. But then we have to drive around them in the directions they allow and not in the directions they prohibit. The same is true for human creations such as language, art, and history. We create the rules and vocabulary of a language, and then are bound to abide by them if we wish to be understood. We write the history of our culture, and then live in the place that our history tells us we have arrived at. We create psychologies that tell us that people are "information-processors," and then talk as if our brain really was a computer. We create the transmission regime of communication and then talk as if we really were sending messages from one mind to another when we communicate. For Dilthey (1894/1976a), the role of psychology is to look to those *creations* of mental processes and not to mental processes in themselves. We must understand our mental lives in the midst of their creations: "In language, myth, literature and art, i.e., in all historical achievements, we have before us mental life which has been, as it were, objectified; they are products of the active mental forces, stable configurations composed of mental constituents and subject to mental laws" (p. 94).

Time and Autobiography

Mental states are not objects located in space. You cannot look inside someone's skull and observe such things. Mental states are processes that take place over time. Therefore, we must understand mental life in terms of a progression and development over time. An emotion, decision, idea, or thought has no intrinsic value. Rather, its value is determined by a consideration of those acts which caused them to come into being, and those acts which they will cause to happen in the future. Dilthey (1894/1976a) describes it this way:

> In the same way as a botanist must first describe the sequence of events from the moment an acorn begins to germinate in the ground to that when one drops from the tree, the psychologist must describe the process of mental structure in terms of the laws of development and the uniformity of succession. (p. 96)

Our experience of time is of a restless progression. The present constantly becomes the past and the future constantly becomes the present. When you get to the end of this paragraph, stop reading and reflect on the present moment you are in. Feel that moment pass and slip into the past. That moment will now only exist as a memory for you. No matter how hard you try to fix your experience on the present moment, it has already slipped away and become a memory of a moment that is now the past.

The constant fluidity of the present makes it difficult, if not impossible, to ever pin down. There never is *a* present. What we experience as the present always contains a memory of what has just been present. We cannot grasp the essence of this experience of the present. We can only reflect upon it once it has passed and, as Dilthey (1906/1976b) noted, that "observation destroys the experience" (p. 210). In fact temporal succession, strictly speaking, cannot be experienced. We experience changes of that which has just been and the fact that these changes have occurred. But we do not experience the flow itself.

Our experience of life, then, is not the experience of the present. That much is impossible. Rather, our experiences of life are the memories of those experiences as they occur in a temporal flow and, more importantly, how those memories are *related* to one another. We understand the present moment with respect to the moment that passed before it. We understand that moment with respect to the moment before that, and so on: "Like a row of houses or trees receding into the distance and becoming smaller the line of memories becomes fainter until the images are lost in the darkness of the horizon" (Dilthey, 1906/1976b, p. 209).

Our understanding of what any particular memory means takes place in a temporal process very much like a conversation. When my student says

"First I have an idea, then I communicate that idea to my friend"

I understand what that utterance means by knowing its place with respect to a number of other utterances which came before it, and to which it would be considered an appropriate response. The utterance has occurred as part of an ongoing temporal stream and its meaning and relevance is determined by its place within that stream, both in terms of the utterances that came before it (the past) and the utterances that it will cause to happen next (the future). For Dilthey, our experience of our mental states consists of experiences that are related to each other in time. It is not the individual thought, utterance, or experience that is important, but how these fit together into an ongoing temporal pattern of experiences. For Dilthey (1906/1976b), "the intrinsic values of the experienced present stand unconnected beside each other; they can only be compared with each other and evaluated" (p. 216). No moment stands in isolation. Any experience can only make sense and have meaning when it is put in relation with other experiences. Dilthey does not ask what a mental state *is*, but rather addresses the *context* in which that state occurs. For a total understanding of any particular idea or event, it is necessary to consider it with respect to the total context of a person's life, the complete temporal stream from birth until death.

It is on the basis of this reasoning that Dilthey advocates the form of the *autobiography* as the highest and most instructive means of the understanding of a life and the events and utterances within that life. Autobiography represents, for Dilthey (1906/1976b), "the roots of all historical comprehension" (p. 215). Autobiography is all about understanding one's self and the meaning of events in one's own life. We understand how events and meanings are related in our own lives through reflection on our autobiographies. We understand why we did this or said that because we know the history that led up to those events and the consequences that arose as a result of them. We also know the relative value of these events in terms of the overall structure of our lives. Some events are very important, such as the first time you asked your future boyfriend on a first date or proposed marriage to your future wife. Other events have less value, such as watching the same episode of *The Simpsons* for the tenth time. To understand any particular event within that life, it is necessary to place it back into the fullness of this stream. Only then will that event have meaning. For example, ask yourself why you are reading this book. Because you're interested in communication? Pain dial up to ninety-five! There is a life-history in which reading this book is an appropriate thing for you to do. Maybe you are a communication student and this has been assigned for a class. There is some sequence of other events, other books, other situations, that have led you to this moment, to you reading this sentence right now. This book and your reading did not happen by accident. It is not a random event. To understand what you are doing now, I would need to know the biography of your life up until this point.

Autobiography is preferable to biography because the person writing the autobiography is the same person who has lived and experienced the life. The autobiographer has intimate knowledge of events and contexts that the biographer could only approximate. The author of an autobiography seeks the connecting threads in the history of her life. In memory, she singles out and accentuates moments that are experienced as significant while others fade into forgetfulness: "from an endless, countless multiplicity what is worth recording has been pre-selected" (Dilthey, 1906/1976b, p. 215). Any particular action or event derives its significance and meaning from its relationship to the totality of the person's life and its place between past and future which can now be charted. However, the autobiographer can never state absolutely what the significance of any event is or will be since the autobiographer's life is still ongoing. One would have to wait until the end of life to grasp its total significance: "for it is only at the hour of death would one survey the whole from which the relationship between the parts could be ascertained" (Dilthey, 1906/1976b, p. 236). I am reminded of here of what Barnett Pearce (1994) has called the "Shotter Strategy" which arose from a conversation Pearce had with communication theorist John Shotter:

> Assume that you are talking about something important to you, and someone asks, "What does that mean?" Shotter suggests that you should reply, "I'm not completely sure yet; we have not finished our conversation." (p. 123)

Pearce and Shotter are suggesting something very similar to Dilthey; the meaning of an utterance cannot be known in isolation, but only with respect to the ongoing stream of other utterances. As long as the stream of utterances remains incomplete, i.e., until the conversation is finished, it will not be possible to state absolutely the meaning or significance of the utterances. For Dilthey, that conversation only ends with the physical demise of the person. There is no hidden meaning that exists apart or behind these conversations which can somehow explain their significance. As Dilthey (1906/1976b) has noted, "life is like a melody the notes of which are not the expression of hidden realities within. Like notes in a melody, life expresses nothing but itself" (p. 237).

Implications for an Understanding of Communication

Dilthey introduces autobiography as a means by which one can understand the meaning and events of our own lives. Communication as a problem emerges in Dilthey's consideration of how we are to understand the actions of other people, including their communicative actions. Since we do not have access to a person's complete biography, how are we to understand the significance of what they are saying to us?

Typically, given our modern immersion in the transmission regime of communication, we seek to understand the actions and utterances of others by reference to the underlying mental states of which they are a sign. But we cannot know these mental states directly. We can only know the inner lives of others through the impact of their gestures, sounds, and acts upon our senses. I can ask you to articulate the ideas that lie behind your words or actions, but your response would simply give me more utterances and actions that I would need to interpret. It is up to *me* to reconstruct the inner source of the signs which I have perceived.

The materials for this reconstruction have to be supplied by transferring them from our own lives. For Dilthey, understanding the utterance of another person follows the same logic as a person making sense of an event in their own autobiography. If you are speaking to me, I need to understand your words in terms of their relationship to the temporal flow of the life in which they play a part. I do not need to understand what actual ideas lie behind your words, although I am free to guess at what these might be. However, I do need to understand where these words fit with respect to the other utterances and actions that comprise a person's life. In other words, I need to place these actions in the context of a life story in which they make sense. Unfortunately, I do not know the life story of the person I am speaking with, at least not all of it to the last detail, so I cannot know with any certainty how the utterances and actions I am perceiving now are related to any actions that occurred in the past. However, I do have access to my own life story. I do have knowledge of similar utterances and actions in my own life and how they are related to other events in my own life story. I can take the knowledge of these relationships and project them onto to the actions of the other people. I now have the context of a life story in which I can interpret and understand the actions of the other person.

I have an in-class exercise where I attempt to demonstrate this principle to my students. I ask five people in the class to stand in front of their colleagues at the front of the room. The five hardy volunteers typically look nervous. They appear shiftless and never quite sure where to look.

Some of the students look at me, others look at the floor or ceiling. I ask the rest of the class to examine the five volunteers very closely. "Take a close look at how they are dressed," I say. "Look at their shoes, their pants, the style of their shirt, that interesting hat. Look closely at their hairstyle. Take a look at how they hold themselves. Are they standing straight? Are they slouched? Are they standing facing you, or turned to the side? Look at what they are doing with their hands."

At this point, the students suddenly become aware of their hands! They fidget nervously, not knowing quite what to do with them. Some thrust their arms straight down to their sides, others fold their arms, some put their hands in their pockets.

"Look at their facial expressions," I continue, mercilessly. "Look at their eyes and where they are looking."

This typically leads to nervous laughter and more defensive body movement. I then ask the students in the class to pick one of the five volunteers and provide answers to the following questions:

- What kind of car does this person drive or would like to drive?
- What vacation spot would this person enjoy most?
- Is this person shy or outgoing at a party?
- What type of music does this person listen to?
- What was the last movie this person saw at the movie theater?

At first, the students protest. "How could I possibly know what kind of car they drive," they say. " I don't know this person." I encourage them to try anyway. I then ask the students to share their answers with the volunteers and the class. This usually leads to much good-humored discussion as they articulate their perceptions of the poor volunteers. What is interesting is not how accurate these perceptions are, although in many cases the perceptions are surprisingly accurate. Rather, what is fascinating is how detailed these perceptions can become. The students are not guessing at all. Rather they articulate a mini life-story in which all the elements they have at their disposal come together. The guy with the plaid shirt and the jeans drives a pickup truck. The girl with the tanned skin and the belly shirt likes to vacation at the beach. The students create a biography in which they can relate the behaviors and their perceptions into a coherent whole. But the story is not the story of the volunteers. It is a story informed by the students' own autobiographies, of how events and behaviors are related together in their own lives. The students' knowledge of their own autobiographies provides a whole in which the particular actions and utterances of others can be located and interpreted.

This relationship between parts and wholes provides the underpinnings of Dilthey's approach to communication. For Dilthey, understanding of words, utterances, or any kind of sign has to be considered as induction. By induction, Dilthey is not referring to the type of reasoning in which a general law is inferred from an incomplete number of cases. Rather, induction for Dilthey refers to a type of reasoning in which one coordinates these cases into a structure or orderly system by treating them as parts of a whole. Every word, sentence, and utterance is both determined and undetermined. Each contains a range of potential meanings depending on the contexts in which they appear. For example, consider the sentence:

My cat is beautiful.

Each word in this sentence has a meaning. By joining the words, we arrive at the meaning of the sentence. There is an interaction between the whole (the sentence) and the parts (the words) through which the ambiguities of meaning are eliminated and the meaning of the individual words determined.

The meaning of the sentence (a part) is likewise determined by its interaction with the text (a whole) in which it appears. By itself, the utterance "My cat is beautiful" is not particularly interesting or enlightening. However, when this utterance is joined with and made to stand in relation to other utterances in a paragraph, or a chapter, or the complete text of this book, your understanding of it becomes much richer. You realize, for instance, that the utterance "My cat is beautiful" does not refer to any specific cat or its attributes at all, not even my daughter's cat. If you are reading my text appropriately, you will understand "My cat is beautiful" to be an example in a chapter intended to articulate Dilthey's account of psychology and communication (or maybe I am using Dilthey's philosophy to talk about my cat, who knows?) In any case, your understanding of "My cat is beautiful" makes no reference to any idea or mental state I may have had in my mind when I wrote this sentence, nor is the existence of any such mental state relevant to your understanding. What is relevant is the place of "My cat is beautiful" in the structure of the overall text and your knowledge of how this utterance is *related* to the utterances that come before and after it, as in a conversation. Dilthey (1906/1976b) makes the same point in terms of watching a play: "If a play is performed, it is not only the naive spectator who is wholly absorbed in the plot without thinking of the author" (p. 224). Understanding is directed toward the plot, the characters, and the interplay of different factors. It is not directed toward trying to guess what was in the author's mind.

The same principle holds for larger units of text. For example, here at chapter eight in this text, you have the benefit of chapters one and two to frame your reading of this paragraph, but not the benefit of chapters eight and nine. It is entirely possible that the text in these later chapters could create a completely different meaning for the material you are reading now. For instance, the title of this chapter is "The Genuine Conversation." What does that mean? You cannot understand this title by trying to guess what's in my head. You need to see how this chapter heading fits into the context of the whole of this chapter. In addition, since you have not reached the end of the chapter yet, you do not have the complete context necessary to formulate an appropriate understanding.

As you, the reader, move through this text for the first time, the contexts for interpretation constantly grow and change. It is entirely possible that this context will shift, develop, and evolve in ways that you, the reader, do not predict. In order to derive the complete meaning of this text, you will have to read it twice; the first time to acquire the full context of the text and the second to read it *within* the totality of the experiential stream. As Eco (1979) points out, "that is why in reading literary texts one is obliged to look backward many times, and, in general, the more complex the text, the more it has to be read twice, and the second time from the end" (p. 26). Arthur Schopenhauer (1818/1969) made the same plea to his readers in the preface to *The World as Will and Representation*:

> No advice can be given other than *to read the book twice*, and to do so the first time with much patience. This patience is to be derived only from the belief, voluntarily accorded, that the beginning presupposes the end almost as much as the end the beginning, and that every earlier part presupposes the later almost as much as the later the earlier. (p. xii)

The point is the same for both Eco and Schopenhauer. Both realize that the end of the text is made meaningful in the context of the text that comes before it. This much is obvious. But Eco and Schopenhauer further suggest that the beginning of a text is made meaningful only in the context of its end.

In this discussion of Dilthey's treatment of time, context, and autobiography with respect to the understanding of others, we can see the contours of a way of speaking about communication that does not require us to make reference to the individual mind. It is not necessary to view communication as the transmission of ideas from one mind to another. Rather, the essence of communication, of understanding what others do and say, is the interpretation and evaluation of communicative acts with respect to the conversational and biographical streams in which it occurs. What we need to describe and understand is not the operations of the mind which produced the utterance, but the temporal stream of utterances which bound it, both in the past and in the future. This notion of speaking about communication in terms of conversational contexts as opposed to a process of transmission is described more fully in the hermeneutics of Hans-Georg Gadamer, which is the subject of the following section.

A Spirit of its Own

Nothing that is said has its truth simply in itself, but refers instead backward and forward to what is unsaid. Every assertion is motivated, that is, one can sensibly ask of everything that is said, "Why did you say that?" (Hans-Georg Gadamer)

Whenever we have our discussions of "What is communication?" my students prize highly their ability to be "in control." If there is one thing that is told to them by the regime of communication, it is that communication skills can be learned which will enable my students to control their behavior and utterances and, more importantly, be able to control the behavior of others. In this final section, I want to explore a hermeneutic discourse of communication that (a) does not require reference to the individual mind, and (b) does not require communication to be spoken of in terms of control.

The discourse I will refer to is that of Hans-Georg Gadamer (1900-2002), a German philosopher whose hermeneutics grew out of his historical and philosophical studies and his abiding interest in literature and poetry. The model of communication proposed by Gadamer is one with which we are all very familiar: the spontaneous conversation. Think about the last time you spoke with a close friend or family member on the telephone. There you are, talking away, and the next thing you know forty-five minutes have gone by, maybe an hour. Where did that time go? It seemed to pass by so quickly. Have you ever had that experience? All of my students certainly have.

So what happened in the forty-five minutes that went by so quickly? Sometimes it is hard to tell. You began by talking about your daughter's performance in the recent school play but, before you know it, you were talking about all kinds of topics: the health of your cat, your upcoming deadline, your sister's bizarre behavior, an old friend who sent you an email out of the blue. Sometimes you find yourself disclosing personal feelings that you never really intended to reveal. As you find yourself moving from one topic to the next, or dwelling on one topic at length, you get the sense

169

that this conversation has taken on a life of its own and you have been caught up in its currents. It takes you to places that you would never have imagined or predicted when the conversation started. It is the experience of a conversation like this that Gadamer refers to as a "genuine conversation" (at last, the inspiration for the title of this chapter is revealed!) Gadamer's description of the genuine conversation is worth quoting in full:

> We say that we "conduct" a conversation, but the more genuine a conversation is, the less its conduct lies within the will of either partner. Thus a genuine conversation is never the one that we wanted to conduct. Rather, it is generally more correct to say that we fall into conversation, or even that we become involved in it. The way one word follows another, with the conversation taking its own twists and reaching its own conclusion, may well be conducted in some way, but the partners conversing are far less the leaders of it than the led. No one knows in advance what will "come out" of a conversation. Understanding or its failure is like an event that happens to us. Thus we can say that something was a good conversation or that it was ill fated. All this shows that a conversation has a spirit of its own, and that the language in which it is conducted bears its own truth within it-i.e., that it allows something to "emerge" which henceforth exists. (Gadamer, 1960/1989, p. 383)

One thing that my students and I can agree on is that it is not intellectually satisfying to describe and explain the experience of a genuine conversation in terms of one mind transmitting ideas to another mind. The experience of the conversation is much more than this. A better metaphor for the genuine conversation is that of a game played by two players who become totally absorbed in its continual back and forth movement. The game is not the action of subjectivity, i.e., what is going on *inside* the players' minds. As Gadamer (1966/1976a) points out, we must "free ourselves from the customary mode of thinking that considers the nature of the game from the point of view of the consciousness of the player" (p. 66). The real subject of playing is the game itself. The game creates its own place and its movements and aims are cut off from direct involvement in the world stretching beyond it. All playing is, in fact, a "being played."

Similarly, in genuine conversation, the interlocutor does not think of what she says before she says it. There is no gap between the thought and utterance. Indeed, Gadamer (1966/1976a) proposes that "no individual has a real consciousness of his speaking when he speaks" (p. 64) and that "when one enters into dialogue with another person and then is carried along further by the dialogue, it is no longer the will of the individual person, holding itself back or exposing itself, that is determinative" (p. 66). Often, the interlocutor is surprised by what she finds herself to be saying. As Gadamer (1962/1976b) proposes that "it cannot be denied that in an actual dialogue of this kind something of the character of accident, favor, and surprise-and, in the end, of buoyancy, indeed, of elevation-that belongs to the nature of the game that is present" (p. 57).

My students are initially incredulous at the claim that their utterances in a conversation are motivated by a game-like environment rather than some mysterious mental process inside their heads. But Gadamer (1960/1989) is very clear on this point: "Understanding is not based on transposing oneself into another person" (p. 383) and further, "to understand what a person says is . . . to come to an understanding about the subject matter, not to get inside another person and relive his experiences" (p. 383). Instead, to understand any given utterance, we don't seek to know the idea *behind* the utterance (this is unknowable to us). We need to understand the nature of the conversational game in which the utterance appears as an appropriate thing to say. As Gadamer (1966/1976a) notes, "nothing that is said has its truth simply in itself, but refers instead backward and forward to what is unsaid" (p. 67). The key to understanding an utterance produced in conversation is not to ask "what do you mean," but rather to ask:

"Why did you say that?" (Gadamer, 1966/1976a, p. 67)

For example, I began this book by describing typical conversations I have had with my students in response to the question "What is communication?" A common response is something like "Communication is the exchange of ideas." Then I ask Gadamer's question:

"Why did you say that?"

I continue: "Did a thought emerge in your mind that you then encoded and transmitted to me by making noise with your larynx?"

The students nod and agree with this analysis, safe in the constraints of the transmission regime of communication. However, there is another way to explain why they said what they did: "Communication is the exchange of ideas" was uttered as a *response to my question*.

"Your utterance was made in response to my utterance," I tell them. "Before I asked the question, *you had no idea* that you were going to say 'Communication is the exchange of ideas.' It was my question that motivated your utterance and brought it into being and *not* an idea in your mind. Your utterance was a logical and appropriate utterance to make in the context of the conversational game in which we are engaged."

The utterance "Communication is the exchange of ideas" is both motivated and constrained by the structure of the evolving conversation. The conversation *motivates* the utterance because it provides the reason for it being uttered at all. The utterance occurs because my question gives it a logical space in which its appearance makes sense. If I had not asked "What is communication?" there would be no reason to blurt out "Communication is the exchange of ideas." On the other hand, the conversation *constrains* what can be said at any given point. When I ask the question "What is communication?" the range of appropriate responses you can give is limited by the question I have asked.

Another challenge I give to my students is this:

"Try to say something that is not bound by the logic of this conversation. Say something to me that is completely original."

The students try. They say things like "Subliminal dogs walk on the moon." To which I reply, in true Gadamerian fashion, "Why did you say that?" The answer, of course, is that the bizarre utterance "Subliminal dogs walk on the moon" is not so bizarre at all. It was uttered *in response* to my request to produce an original statement. My students still continue to cling to the notion that "Subliminal dogs walk on the moon" is a product of their minds. But, of course, it is not. The reason for their producing the utterance "Subliminal dogs walk on the moon" is not to be found in some dark place in their heads. The motivation for this utterance is quite open and public in the structures of the conversation that involves both of us. It is simply impossible for my students to do or say *anything* that does not fall into a pattern created for them by the conversation. As Gadamer (1960/1989) wrote in his description of the genuine conversation, "the way one word follows another, with the conversation taking its own twists and reaching its own conclusion, may well be conducted in some way, but the partners conversing are far less the leaders of it than the led" (p. 383).

My students usually feel very agitated at this point. They can sense the rug of the transmission regime slowly being pulled from beneath their feet. The claim that their communication behavior is the result of their being led by a conversational structure that is *outside* of themselves, rather than inside, is totally unacceptable to them. But it is here that Gadamer forces us to go. Gadamer (1966/1976a) is very forceful in his assertion that "speaking does not belong in the sphere of the 'I' but in the sphere of the 'We'" (p. 65). The communication behaviors displayed in a genuine conversation are not the products of your mind or my mind working individually. Our acts of communication are co-created by both of us acting and reacting to each other's utterances, with each utterance creating the conditions for the next one to follow. What we say is not determined by what is inside our minds, but where we are in the sequence of the conversation.

I further challenge my students to say something original and spontaneous in a situation outside of this particular language game in the classroom situation. I tell them: "Go home and say something bizarre over dinner, or in front of your girlfriend." Of course, the first thing your girlfriend will ask is "Why did you say that?" What motivated you to, all of a sudden, say "Subliminal dogs walk on the moon?" Gadamer would have been proud of your girlfriend! If you answer truthfully, you will have to say that you were in a class with this crazy Professor Radford who challenged you to say something original in front of your girlfriend. Of course, this so called "original" utterance may seem strange in the new context, but it still makes perfect sense in terms of the conversation that occurred in class. It is still motivated by a conversational structure. It is not the product of some internal brain process.

Like Dilthey and Husserl, Gadamer recognizes that understanding is a problem of understanding messages, not people. When you read this book, you understand the words before you on the page. You do not understand *me*, the author. Understanding is not about recreating the state of mind of another person. It is not about guessing my intentions. Instead, we have described communication in a manner that does not depend at all on the assumptions of the transmission regime. Understanding these words is less about understanding me and the flow of ideas from my mind to yours. It is about understanding yourself and the relationship you have with this text. You do not receive meaning *from* the text. You create meaning as you engage *with* the text. The text comes alive in the context of this engagement. As Gadamer (1962/1976b) tells us, this text "does not simply speak its words, always the same, in lifeless rigidity, but gives ever new answers to the person who questions it and poses ever new questions to him who answers it. To understand a text is to come to understand oneself in a kind of dialogue" (Gadamer, 1962/1976b, p. 57). Your reading of this book is not an instance of transmission, but an example of conversation.

Nine
Towards a New Way of Speaking About Communication:
It All Happens Out There

Remember Gary, nothing happens in here. It all happens out there. (Rom Harre)

You must climb out through my sentences; then you will see the world correctly. (Ludwig Wittgenstein)

I would like to conclude this book by recalling a brief but very memorable encounter I had with Dr. Rom Harre in 1989. Rom Harre is a very distinguished professor of psychology most well known for his development of a hermeneutic account of human behavior (see Harre & Secord, 1972). I'm sure Dr. Harre does not remember this encounter and he may be surprised to learn what a profound impact he had on a young mind attempting to make sense of communication. I was a doctoral student at the time and I was giving my first presentation at a national academic conference (Radford, 1989). My topic was subliminal perception. However, I was not concerned with speculating on the nature of the mind which would enable messages presented below the threshold of awareness to be perceived, decoded, and acted upon. I wanted to know how it was we *talked* about subliminal perception as a phenomenon in the real world, and why it had value to the people who spoke about it. What purposes did such talk serve? What practical value did it have for the people who used it? What role did it play in our discursive construction of the human mind as an information-processing system?

Dr. Harre approached me afterwards. He shook my hand and thanked me for giving my paper. I was somewhat awestruck and honored that Dr. Harre would take the time to speak to me after the session. Then he said something to me that has stayed with me until this very day:

"Remember Gary, nothing happens in here," he said, pointing to his head. He then unfolded his palm and performed a wide, sweeping gesture. "It all happens out there," he said.

Dr. Harre's words struck me, not because they were particularly profound, but rather because they were being said to me by Dr. Rom Harre, one of the most respected thinkers on these topics in the world. My encounter with Dr. Harre was a pivotal moment for me. It totally changed the course of my thinking about communication and set in motion my academic career that was to follow. This encounter was my "Do it to Julia!" moment. In one simple phrase, Dr. Harre produced within me a complete gestalt switch in the way I saw communication. The duck was gone and a rabbit's head stood in its place. My understanding of communication finally and completely became unmoored from the transmission regime and was set adrift in a discourse that I had yet to understand.

Of course, I understood perfectly well that it was possible to see communication as the product of a discursive regime in a detached and speculative way. My conference paper and my ongoing doctoral dissertation were both based on the writings of Michel Foucault. Foucault's arguments were slowly beginning to make sense to me and I enjoyed the challenge and the interpretive effort required to understand them. But at the end of the day, the reality of the transmission regime would always come back into focus and my words were once again the products of my ideas. Reading and writing about Foucault was interesting and a means to completing my Ph.D. work, but it did not provide the foundation upon which to base my comprehension of reality. I had the transmission regime for that, along with everybody else (not that we saw it as a discursive regime of course-this *was* reality).

But my encounter with Dr. Harre had the bizarre effect of snapping me into a view of communication based on discourse rather than mental processes. Since that time I have not been able to snap back again. Maybe it was something to do with the situation. Maybe my senses were heightened due to the extreme nervousness I felt at presenting my first conference paper. Maybe it was the awe I felt at being approached by Rom Harre. Maybe the situation was similar to that of Winston Smith with the rat cage strapped to his face in Room 101, heart and mind racing, when "Do it to Julia!" really did make sense to him. In that brief encounter, I knew in a manner that would be destined to shape the nature of my reality that "Nothing happens in here. It all happens out there."

I understood completely that the psychology of information-processing was not an appropriate discourse to describe the conversations we have everyday. Even as I was learning the psychological discourse of communication during my undergraduate years at Sheffield Hallam University, I had an inkling that something was not quite right. But I had no other language to turn to in order to scratch that itch. Without the appropriate linguistic resources, I had no choice but to operate in a reality dominated by the transmission regime of communication. But after my brief encounter with Dr. Harre, I suddenly found the confidence to believe that the transmission regime was a *language*. Not a language that *described* a separate reality, but a language that *constituted* a reality. Harre's words brought into sharp focus that the reality of communication was not to be found "in here," in the ontology of unconscious information-processing routines. Communication could also be found "out there," in language, in the way we talk. To understand communication, we must understand the *language of communication* and the genuine conversations in which such language is created and used.

Harre's remark has inspired me over these years to continue my possibly thankless task of convincing my students that it is possible to talk about communication without invoking terms such as "idea," "thought," or "information processing." My first task is to have the students consider words such as "thought" and "idea" in terms of what they really are: words that appear in sentences that are themselves part of texts. For example:

"I think you look nice today."
"I thought I would have a hot dog instead of a salad for lunch."
"I thought hard about what I would write for my assignment."

Just because you use a word like "thought" in your everyday conversations does not mean it actually refers to some real process. That is an inferential leap that you are making based on a particular knowledge and use of language. You read the sentence "I think you look nice today" in the same way you read any other sentence in this book. When you tell your friend that you think her new sweater looks really classy, you are producing a text for her to read and make sense of. In none of these cases is it necessary for some objective process of thought production in the sender to be present and real to make sense of these sentences. They could just as well have been written by a machine (as indeed was common in the society envisaged by Orwell in *1984*). Wittgenstein's narrative of a person trying to observe their own thoughts using an MRI machine demonstrates that getting a grip on the real object that the term "thought" refers to is difficult, if not impossible. So "thought" is just a word used in conversations. It plays a role in certain texts and narratives, and not in others. If we behave "as if" we really did have these "thoughts" (which my students cannot locate, describe, or experience), then that is a choice we have made with the help of our discursive regime of communication. But we can communicate and operate equally well without having to invoke "thoughts" or "ideas" in our discourse.

"Language," Gadamer (1960/1989) writes, "is not one of man's possessions in the world; rather, on it depends the fact that man has a *world* at all" (p. 443). After my encounter with Harre, I came to understand that there is no such thing as a "world-in-itself" that lies beyond all language. The idea of the "world-in-itself" is itself a linguistic creation. "The world-in-itself," or "the real world," or "reality" are all parts of language that express a particular point of view. Likewise, there is no such thing as "communication" that lies beyond the language of the transmission regime. Regardless of whatever language we use to talk about communication, we can never succeed in seeing anything other than an ever more extended aspect of the subject. Wittgenstein wrote that "*the boundary of my language is the boundary of my world*" (Kolak, 1998, p. 37). Similarly Gadamer (1960/1989) writes that "language can do all this because it is not a creation of reflective thought, but itself helps to fashion the world orientation in which we live" (p. 450). We believe that we live in a "real world" because our language provides us with that view, and not the other way around. Language is less like a tool that we pick up and use to achieve our individual aims, and more like an environment which shapes our collective behaviors through the game-like patterns of genuine conversation.

For example, consider the situation of a newborn child. The child is born into a language community that exists independently of her. It existed when she arrived. It will continue to exist after she is gone. Through her immersion in language, the child is introduced to a particular orientation and relationship to the world. It is not simply the case that a child learns a language to name things, whether these things be objects in the world or mental states in her head. Young children are *absorbed* into ongoing game-like patterns of social interaction not of their own making. They have tremendous abilities to find *places* in these games and to use language in appropriate ways. They learn appropriate sounds, movements, and gestures *in response* to the movements of their mothers and fathers. The child makes a facial expression, the father laughs, and the child laughs in response. The mother is playing peek-a-boo. She makes a strange face and a high-pitched sound. The child laughs in response. The mother smiles in response to her child. In these series of mutually interdependent actions and responses, the behavior of parent and child becomes linked and coordinated. Language is developed in the same manner; not as repetition, but as appropriate acts to make in the context of these conversational games.

We do not have to teach children how to engage in game-like patterns of action. However, the specific games they find teach them many things about who they are and the range of possible relationships they can have with others. It is within the context of these conversations that the infant develops schemas of the human face, voice, and touch. It learns how to place these perceptions within relational contexts. It learns the meaning of a smile from its place within a conversational context, of how it fits within a stream of other behaviors and responses. The child learns to participate in the temporal patterning of human behavior and the meaning of different changes and variation in tempo and rhythm. She learns the social cues and conventions that are effective in initiating, maintaining, terminating, and avoiding interactions with her mother. When mothers talk to babies, they continually embed their babies in a conversation in which the baby is treated as if it had a full complement of moral and intellectual qualities. The mother never reacts to the baby as a kind of empty vessel. She reacts to the baby as if she has been transformed psychologically by the conversational pattern. She treats the baby as if it had the moral and psychological attributes which she ascribes to it through her talk. The mother does not talk *about* her baby's intentions; she provides the baby with them, and then she reacts to the baby as if it had them. It is not the case that the child learns a language, but rather that the language finds a place for the child, within existing contexts of language games, of conversations.

But even after all of these observations about the behaviors of young children coupled with the profound insights of scholars such as Umberto Eco, Edmund Husserl, Wilhelm Dilthey, Hans-Georg Gadamer, and Rom Harre, there is still something strange about this way of viewing our relationship to language. We may accept totally Gadamer's (1960/1989) assertion that "language speaks us, rather than we speak it" (p. 463). But, as we go about our daily lives, it certainly does not feel like we are being spoken by language. Gadamer's proposition seems more like an exotic philosophical pronouncement than a description of reality. The problem, of course, is that the reality to which we compare Gadamer's statement is itself constructed in language. As Gadamer (1960/1989) notes:

> Our verbal experience of the world is prior to everything that is recognized and addressed as existing. *That language and world are related in a fundamental way does not mean, then, that world becomes the object of language.* Rather, the object of knowledge and statements is already enclosed within the world horizon of language. (p. 450)

John Shotter (1993) characterizes the situation as follows:

> Conversation is a kind of ultimate reality for us. We cannot turn it around to understand its nature in terms of particular models, theories, rules, or conventions, for, unless we can discuss such entities conversationally, we have no way of justifying to each other that we are indeed applying them aright. Thus they cannot themselves be a prior condition for such joint discussions; rather they must be a consequence of them. (p. 459)

To understand the nature of communication as conversation requires us to do something that seems contradictory. We need to engage in a conversation about the nature of conversation. We need to communicate to each other about our ability to communicate to each other. I need to write to a text to describe how it is possible to communicate through a text. In order to understand and breach the transmission regime as a form of discourse, we must use conversation as both our subject matter and our tool. We must *speak* about communication in a different way. The transmission regime only achieves its reality for us because of its place in the language games of genuine conversations. We must come to realize that the *practice* of conversation supercedes all of the discourses in which our realities are constituted. Faced with these realizations, we will eventually find ourselves in the predicament of Winston Smith slowly coming to his realization that the discourse that holds his world and himself together is formed in a process of conversation that he now has no control over:

> [O'Brien's] voice had grown almost dreamy. The exaltation, the lunatic enthusiasm, was still in his face. He is not pretending, thought Winston; he is not a hypocrite; he believes every word he says. What most oppressed him was the consciousness of his own intellectual inferiority. He watched the heavy yet graceful

form strolling to and fro, in and out of his range of vision. O'Brien was a being in all ways larger than himself. There was no idea that had ever had, or could have, that O'Brien had not long ago known, examined, and rejected. His mind *contained* Winston's mind. But in that case how could it be true that O'Brien was mad? It must be he, Winston, who was mad. (Orwell, 1949, p. 211)

Are you feeling like Winston? Is your transmission view of communication really tantamount to madness? In certain language games, it certainly could be. But this is no easy task. Gadamer (1960/1989) noted that "the consciousness of being conditioned does not supercede our conditionedness" (p. 448). The knowledge that our reality is conditioned by our immersion in language does not prevent us from experiencing the reality that language provides for us. Gadamer (1960/1989) states that "we can keep seeing things a certain way while at the same time knowing that doing so is absurd in the world of understanding" (p. 449). For example, to our vision, the setting sun is a reality. We can watch it move behind the horizon. By constructing a model in which the Earth revolves around the sun, we can mentally liberate ourselves from the evidence of our senses, and we can rationally view things from the perspective of Copernicus. But we cannot try to supercede or refute natural appearances by viewing things through the eyes of scientific understanding. We may "know" that the Earth moves and the sun is still, but we still "see" the sun moving beyond the horizon as it sets.

The same is true with respect to our immersion in a transmission regime of communication. No matter how much we are exposed to the theories of such scholars as Umberto Eco, Edmund Husserl, Wilhem Dilthey, and Hans-Georg Gadamer, we still continue to experience communication according to the Lockean view since this is the language game into which we have been immersed. It has been woven into the language games of our lives since our childhood. It is part of our common sense understanding of how things are, and it is this understanding that comprises the reality of the world we live in. What we say about communication has genuine reality for us. It is not that the word "communication" refers to a specific concept or act. It accesses a complete picture of reality:

Every word breaks forth as if from a center and is related to a whole, through which alone it is a word. Every word causes the whole of the language to which it belongs to resonate and the whole world-view that underlies it to appear. (Gadamer, 1960/1989, p. 458)

In closing, I do not intend or expect this short book to change the nature of the reality you live in. As you read these final paragraphs, you may find the claim that "communication" is the product of a particular language game I have termed, following Grossberg (1997), the "regime of communication" to be interesting, perhaps even intriguing. But it is not enough to shake your reality that the words on this page have somehow transmitted an idea from my mind and created an idea in your mind. Changing your understanding of communication would require changing the nature of the language games in which "communication" is used as a term, and this text does not have enough power to do that by itself. O'Brien was able to achieve this goal because he could control completely the language games in which Winston attempted, in vain, to articulate a coherent discourse of autonomous thoughts, feelings, and memories. I cannot do this. There are simply too many conversations in your life in which communication is constituted by the transmission regime.

However, something significant has happened here. You have read to the end of this book. The significance of the book should not be measured in terms of whether or not you "believe" what I have said, or if my text has "persuaded" you to adopt its thesis. The book will become significant if it comes to play a role in your conversations from this point forward. Speaking about communication will not change your world overnight. But if you continue to read texts like this one, there will come a moment similar to Winston's cry of "Do it to Julia!" or Rom Harre telling me "It is all out there." Suddenly everything will change and, like Winston, you will come to love Big Brother despite everything you have ever said or believed in the past. I hope you will be prepared to accept such a moment and I hope this text will help you make a short step towards it. In that spirit, I end with the following words from Ludwig Wittgenstein (Kolak, 1998, p. 49). Think about them with the transmission regime of communication in mind:

My sentences are illuminating in the following way: to understand me you must recognize my sentences-once you have climbed out through them, on them, over them-as senseless. (You must, so to speak, throw away the ladder after you have climbed up on it.)

You must climb out through my sentences; then you will see the world correctly.

References

Bergson, M. (1913, October 30). The birth of the dream. *The Independent.*

Berkeley, G. (1975). *A treatise concerning the principles of human knowledge.* In M. R. Ayers (Ed.), *Philosophical works including the works on vision* (pp. 71-153). London, England: Everyman. (Original work published 1710)

Berlo, D. K. (1960). *The process of communication: An introduction to theory and practice.* New York, NY: Holt, Rinehart, Winston.

Bineham, J. L. (1988). A historical account of the hypodermic model in mass communication. *Communication Monographs, 55,* 230-246.

Bowen, F. (1889). *Modern philosophy from Descartes to Schopenhauer and Hartmann* (6th Edition). New York, NY: Charles Scribner's Sons.

Bradby, M. K. (1920). *The logic of the unconscious mind.* London, England: Oxford Medical Publications.

Broadbent, D. E. (1958). *Perception and communication.* London, England: Pergamon.

Bronowski, J. (1973). *The ascent of man.* Boston, MA: Little, Brown and Company.

Carey, J. W. (1977). Mass communication research and cultural studies: An American view. In J. Curran, M. Gurevitch, and J. Woollacott (Eds.), *Mass communication and society.* London, England: Edward Arnold.

Carey, J. W. (1992). Communication as culture: Essays on media and society. New York, NY: Routledge.

Cherry, E. C. (1953). Some experiments on the recognition of speech, with one and with two ears. *Journal of the Acoustical Society of America, 25,* 975-979.

Darnoi, D. N. K. (1967). *The unconscious and Eduard Von Hartmann: A historico-critical monograph.* The Hague, The Netherlands: Martinus Nijhoff.

Deetz, S. A. (1977). Interpretive research in communication: A hermeneutic foundation. *Journal of Communication Inquiry, 3,* 53-69.

Deetz, S. A. and Stevenson, S. L. (1986). *Managing interpersonal communication.* New York, NY: Harper and Row.

Descartes, R. (1960). *Discourse on the method of rightly conducting the reason and seeking truth in the field of science.* In *Discourse on method and meditations* (L. J. Lafleur, Trans.) (pp. 1-57). New York, NY: Macmillan. (Original work published 1637)

References

Descartes, R. (1984). *Meditations on first philosophy*. In *The philosophical writings of Descartes: Volume two* (J. Cottingham, R. Stoothoff, & D. Murdoch, Trans.) (pp. 1-62). Cambridge, England: Cambridge University Press. (Original work published 1641)

Dewey, J. (1958). *Experience and nature*. New York, NY: Dover Publications. (Original work published 1929)

Dilthey, W. (1976a). Ideas about a descriptive and analytical psychology (H. P. Rickman, Trans.). In H. P. Rickman (Ed.), *Dilthey: Selected writings* (pp. 88-97). New York, NY: Cambridge University Press. (Original work published 1894)

Dilthey, W. (1976b). The construction of the historical world in the human studies (H. P. Rickman, Trans.). In H. P. Rickman (Ed.), *Dilthey: Selected writings* (pp. 170-245). New York, NY: Cambridge University Press. (Original work published 1906)

Dixon, N. F. (1971). *Subliminal perception: The nature of a controversy*. London, England: McGraw-Hill.

Dixon, N. F. (1981). *Preconscious processing*. London, England: Wiley.

Dreyfus, H. L. and Rabinow, P. (1983). *Michel Foucault: Beyond structuralism and hermeneutics* (2nd. ed.). Chicago, IL: University of Chicago Press.

Eco, U. (1976). *A theory of semiotics*. Bloomington, IN: Indiana University Press.

Eco, U. (1979). *The role of the reader: Explorations in the semiotics of texts*. Bloomington, IN: Harcourt Brace Jovanovich.

Eco, U. (1983). *Postscript to The Name of the Rose* (W. Weaver, Trans.). New York, NY: Harcourt Brace Jovanovich.

Eco, U. (1989). Openness, information, communication (A. Cancogni, Trans.). In Umberto Eco, *The open work* (pp. 44-83). Cambridge, MA: Harvard University Press.

Eco, U. (1992). *Interpretation and overinterpretation*. Cambridge, England: Cambridge University Press.

Eco, U. (1994). *Six walks in the fictional woods*. Cambridge, MA: Harvard University Press.

Eden, M. (1983). Cybernetics. In F. Machlup and U. Mansfield (Eds.), *The study of information: Interdisciplinary messages*. New York, NY: Wiley.

Elias, P. (1983). Cybernetics: Past and present, east and west.In F. Machlup and U. Mansfield (Eds.), *The study of information: Interdisciplinary messages*. New York, NY: Wiley.

Fechner, G. (1966). *Elements of psychophysics: volume one*. (H. E. Adler, Trans.) (D. H. Howes and E. G. Boring, Eds.). New York, NY: Holt, Rinehart and Winston. (Original work published 1860)

Foucault, M. (1973). *The order of things: An archeology of the human sciences*. New York, NY: Vintage Books. (Original work published 1966)

Foucault, M. (1980). *The history of sexuality. Volume One: An introduction* (R. Hurley, Trans.). New York, NY: Vintage Books. (Original work published 1976)

References

Foucault, M. (1988). The masked philosopher (A. Sheridan, Trans.). In L. D. Kritzman (Ed.), *Michel Foucault: Politics, philosophy, culture. Interviews and other writings, 1977-1984* (pp. 323-330). New York, NY: Routledge.

Freud, S. (1965). *The interpretation of dreams* (8th Edition) (J. Strachey, Trans.). New York, NY: Avon Books. (Original work published 1900; 8th edition published 1930)

Fuller, R. C. (1986). *Americans and the unconscious*. Oxford, England: Oxford University Press.

Gadamer, H-G. (1976a). Man and language (D. E. Linge, Trans.). In D. E. Linge (Ed.), *Philosophical hermeneutics* (pp. 59-68). Berkeley, CA: University of California Press. (Original work published 1966)

Gadamer, H-G. (1976b). On the problem of self-understanding (D. E. Linge, Trans.). In D. E. Linge (Ed.), *Philosophical hermeneutics* (pp. 44-58). Berkeley, CA: University of California Press. (Original work published 1962)

Gadamer, H-G. (1989). *Truth and method* (2nd revised edition) (J. Weinsheimer & D. Marshall, Trans.). New York, NY: Continuum. (Original work published 1960)

Gauld, A. (1968). *The founders of psychical research*. New York, NY: Schocken Books.

Gauld, A. and Shotter, J. D. (1977). *Human action and its psychological investigation*. London, England: Routledge and Kegan Paul.

Giorgi, A. (1970). *Psychology as a human science: A phenomenologically based approach*. New York, NY: Harper and Row.

Glass, A. L., Holyoak, K. J., and Santa, J. L. (1979). *Cognition*. Reading, MA: Addison-Wesley.

Goodman, M. B. (1984). *Write to the point: Effective communication in the workplace*. Englewood Cliffs, NJ: Prentice-Hall.

Gregory, R. L. (Ed.) (1987). *The Oxford companion to the mind*. Oxford, England: Oxford University Press.

Grossberg, L. (1997). *Bringing it all back home: Essays on cultural studies*. Durham, NC: Duke University Press.

Gurney, E., Myers, F. W. H., and Podmore, F. (1970). *Phantasms of the living* (Facsimile reproduction with an introduction by L. R. N. Ashley). Gainesville, FL: Scholars Facsimilies and Reprints. (Original work published 1886)

Hall, G. S. (1912). *Founders of modern psychology*. New York, NY: D. Appleton and Company.

Harre, R., Clarke, D., and De Carlo, N. (1985). *Motives and mechanisms: An introduction to the psychology of action*. London, England: Methuen.

Harre, R. and Secord, P. F. (1972). *The explanation of social behavior*. Totowa, NJ: Rowman and Littlefield.

Hartmann, E. von (1931). *Philosophy of the unconscious: Speculative results according to the inductive method of physical science* (Ninth German Edition) (W. C. Coupland, Trans.). New York, NY: Harcourt, Brace and Company. (Original work published 1884)

References

Hewes, D. E. and Planalp, S. (1987). The individual's place in communication science. In C. R. Berger & S. H. Chaffee (Eds.), *Handbook of communication science* (pp. 146-183). Newbury Park, CA: Sage.

Hickson, M. and Stacks, D. W. (1993). Teaching the introductory communication theory course to undergraduates. *Communication Quarterly, 41*(3), 261-268.

Hovland, C., Janis, I. L., and Kelley, H. H. (1953). *Communication and persuasion: Psychological studies of opinion change.* New Haven, CT: Yale University Press.

Hunt, M. (1982). *The universe within: A new science explores the human mind.* New York, NY: Simon and Schuster.

Husserl, E. (1970). *Logical investigations* (J. N. Findlay, Trans.). New York, NY: Humanities Press. (Original work published 1900)

James, W. (1950). *The principles of psychology* (Volume One). New York, NY: Dover Publications. (Original work published 1890)

James, W. (1958). *The varieties of religious experience.* New York, NY: Mentor Books. (Original work published 1902)

Kant, I. (1965). *The critique of pure reason* (N. Kemp Smith, Trans.). New York, NY: St. Martin's Press. (Original work published 1781)

Klapper, J. T. (1960). *The effects of the mass media.* Glencoe, IL: Free Press.

Klein, D. B. (1979). *The unconscious: Invention or discovery? A historico-critical inquiry.* Santa Monica, CA: Goodyear Publishing Co.

Kochen, M. (1983). Cybernetics in the information disciplines. In F. Machlup and U. Mansfield (Eds.), *The study of information: Interdisciplinary messages.* New York, NY: Wiley.

Kolak, D. (1998). *Wittgenstein's Tractatus.* Mountain View, CA: Mayfield Publishing Company.

Kuhn, T. S. (1970). *The structure of scientific revolutions.* Chicago, IL: University of Chicago Press.

Lasswell, H. D. (1948). The structure and function of communication in society. In L. Bryson (Ed.), *The communication of ideas: A series of addresses.* New York, NY: Harper and Brothers.

Lazarus, R. S. and McCleary, R. A. (1951). Autonomic discrimination without awareness: A study of subception. *Psychological Review, 58,* 113-122.

Libet, B. (1996). Neural processes in the production of conscious experience. In M. Velmans (Ed.), *The science of consciousness: Psychological, neuropsychological, and clinical reviews.* London, England: Routledge.

Linge, D. E. (1976). Editor's introduction. In H-G. Gadamer, *Philosophical hermeneutics* (D. E. Linge, Ed. and Trans.) (pp. xi-lviii). Berkeley, CA: University of California Press.

Lipps, T. (1897). Der begriff des unbewussten in der psychologie. *Records of the Third International Congress in Psychology,* 650-652.

Locke, J. (1975). *An essay concerning human understanding* (P. H. Nidditch, Ed.). Oxford, England: Clarendon Press. (Original work published 1690)

Lodge, O. (1909). *The survival of man: A study in unrecognized human faculty.* New York, NY: Moffat, Yard and Co.

References

Loftus, E. F. (1972). Nouns, adjectives, and semantic memory. *Journal of Experimental Psychology, 96*(1), 213-215.

Loftus, E. F. (1973). Category dominance, instance dominance, and categorization time. Journal of Experimental Psychology, 97(1), 70-74.

Loftus, E. F. (1975). Leading questions and the eyewitness report. *Cognitive Psychology, 7,* 560-572.

Loftus, E. F. (1979a). *Eyewitness testimony.* Cambridge, MA: Harvard University Press.

Loftus, E. F. (1979b). The malleability of human memory. *American Scientist, 67*(3), 312-320.

Loftus, E. F. (1980). *Memory: Surprising new insights into how we remember and why we forget.* Reading, MA: Addision-Wesley.

Loftus, E. F. (1981). Natural and unnatural cognition. *Cognition, 10*(1-3), 193-196.

Loftus, E. F. (1982). Memory and its distortions. *G. Stanley Hall Lecture Series, 2,* 119-154.

Loftus, E. F., Altman, D. and Geballe, R. (1975). Effects of questioning upon a witness' later recollections. *Journal of Police Science and Administration, 3*(2), 162-165.

Loftus, E. F. and Cole, W. (1974). Retrieving attribute and name information from semantic memory. *Journal of Experimental Psychology, 102*(6), 1116-1122.

Loftus, E. F., Freedman, J. L. and Loftus, G. R. (1970), Retrieval of words from subordinate and superordinate categories in semantic hierarchies, *Psychonomic Science, 21*(4), 235-236.

Loftus, E. F. and Freedman, J. L. (1972). Effect of category name frequency on the speed of naming an instance of the category. *Journal of Verbal Learning and Verbal Behavior, 11*(3), 343-347.

Loftus, E. F. and Greene, E. (1980). Warning: Even memory for faces may be contagious. *Law and Human Behavior, 4*(4), 323-334.

Loftus, E. F. and Grober, E. H. (1973). Retrieval from semantic memory by young children. *Developmental Psychology, 8*(2), 310.

Loftus, E. F. and Ketcham, K. (1991). *Witness for the defense: The accused, the eyewitness, and the expert who puts memory on trial.* New York, NY: St. Martin's Press.

Loftus, E. F. and Loftus, G. R. (1974). Changes in memory structure and retrieval over the course of instruction. *Journal of Educational Psychology, 66*(3), 315-318.

Loftus, E. F. & Loftus, G. R. (1976). *Human memory: The processing of information.* Hillsdale, NJ: Erlbaum.

Loftus, E. F. and Loftus, G. R. (1980). On the permanence of stored information in the human brain. *American Psychologist, 35*(5), 409-420.

Loftus, E. F. and Palmer, J. C. (1974). Reconstruction of automobile destruction: An example of the interaction between language and memory. *Journal of Verbal Learning and Verbal Behavior, 13*(5), 585-589.

Loftus, E. F. and Schooler, J. W. (1985). Information-processing conceptualizations of human cognition: Past, present and future. In Brent .D. Ruben (Ed.), *Information and behavior: Volume one.* New Brunswick, NJ: Transaction.

References

Loftus, E. F. and Suppes, P. (1972). Structural variables that determine the speed of retrieving words from long-term memory. *Journal of Verbal Learning and Verbal Behavior, 11*(6), 770-777.

Loftus, E. F., Wiksten, S. and Abelson, R. P. (1974). Using semantic memory to find vs create a mood. *Memory and Cognition, 2*(3), 479-483.

Lucas, S. E. (1995). *The art of public speaking* (5th edition). New York, NY: McGraw Hill.

Marcel, A. J. (1983). Conscious and unconscious processing: Experiments on visual masking and word recognition. *Cognitive Psychology, 15*, 197-237.

Miller, G. A. (1983). The background to modern psychology. In J. Miller (Ed.), *States of mind.* New York, NY: Pantheon.

Munsterberg, H. (1910). Subconscious phenomena. In H. Munsterberg, T. Ribot, P. Janet, J. Jastrow, B. Hart, and M. Prince, *Subconscious phenomena.* Boston, MA: Gorham Press.

Murphy, G. and Ballou, R. O. (1973). *William James on psychical research.* Clifton, NJ: Augustus M. Kelly Publishers.

Myers, F. W. H. (1976). General characteristics of subliminal messages. In F. W. H. Myers, *The subliminal consciousness.* New York, NY: Arno Press. (Original work published 1891)

Neisser, U. (1967). *Cognitive psychology.* New York, NY: Appleton-Century-Crofts.

Nidditch, P. H. (1975). Foreword. In John Locke, *An essay concerning human understanding* (P. H. Nidditch, Ed.). Oxford, England: Clarendon Press.

NIMH. (1982). Violence and aggression. In *Television and behavior: Volume one.* Washington, DC: US Government.

Nolan, C. (1999). *Memento: A screenplay.* Retrieved November 26, 2002, from http://www.moviemalls.com/papers/memento-script.doc

Northridge, W.L. (1924). *Modern theories of the unconscious.* London, England: Kegan Paul, Trench, Trubner and Co.

Orwell, G. (1984). *1984.* New York, NY: Signet. (Original work published 1949)

Oxford English Dictionary - Volume II (1933). Oxford, England: Clarendon Press.

Page, J., Jones, J. P., and Bonham, J. (1969). Communication breakdown [Recorded by Led Zeppelin]. On *Led Zeppelin* [Vinyl Record]. New York, NY: Atlantic Recording Corporation.

Pearce, W. B. (1994). *Interpersonal communication: Making social worlds.* New York, NY: Harper Collins.

Peters, J. D. (1986). Institutional sources of intellectual poverty in communication research. *Communication Research, 13*(4), 527-559.

Peters, J. D. (1989). John Locke, the individual, and the origin of communication. *The Quarterly Journal of Speech, 75*(4), 387-399.

Pilotta, J. J. and Mickunas, A. (1990). *Science of communication: Its phenomenological foundation.* Hillsdale, NJ: Lawrence Erlbaum Associates.

Prince, M. (1921). *The unconscious: The fundamentals of human personality normal and abnormal* (2nd. ed.). New York, NY: Macmillan.

References

Radford, G. P. (1989). *The subliminal discourse: A Foucauldian analysis of a controversy in psychology.* Presented at the Tenth Annual Conference on Discourse Analysis, Temple University, Philadelphia, PA (March 16-19, 1989).

Radford, G. P. (2003). *On Eco.* Belmont, CA: Wadsworth.

Reddy, M. J. (1979). The conduit metaphor-A case of frame conflict in our language about language. In A. Ortony (Ed.), *Metaphor and thought* (pp. 284-324). Cambridge, England: Cambridge University Press.

Richards, G. (1992). *Mental machinery: The origins and consequences of psychological ideas. Part 1: 1600-1850.* Baltimore, MD: John Hopkins University Press.

Ricoeur, P. (1974). Existence and hermeneutics. In P. Ricoeur, *The conflict of interpretations: Essays in hermeneutics.* Evanston, Il: Northwestern University Press.

Rogers, E. M. (1986). *Communication technology: The new media in society.* New York, NY: Free Press.

Rogers, E. M. & Valente, T. W. (1993). A history of information theory in communication research. In J. R. Schement & B. D. Ruben (Eds.), *Between communication and information. Information and behavior: Volume four.* New Brunswick, NJ: Transaction.

Rorty, R. (1989). *Contingency, irony, and solidarity.* Cambridge, England: Cambridge University Press.

Rorty, R. (1992). The pragmatist's progress. In Umberto Eco, *Interpretation and overinterpretation* (pp. 89-108). Cambridge, England: Cambridge University Press.

Saltus, E. E. (1885). *The philosophy of disenchantment.* Boston, MA: Houghton, Mifflin and Company.

Schopenhauer, A. (1969). *The world as will and representation* (Volume 1) (E. J. F. Payne, Trans.). New York, NY: Dover Publications. (Original work published 1818)

Schramm, W. (1954). How communication works. In W. Schramm (Ed.), *The process and effects of mass communication.* Urbana, IL: University of Illinois Press.

Searle, J. R. (1984). *Minds, brains, and science.* Cambridge, MA: Harvard University Press.

Shannon, C. E. (1949). The mathematical theory of communication. In C. E. Shannon and W. Weaver, *The mathematical theory of communication* (pp. 29-125). Urbana, IL: University of Illinois Press.

Shannon, C. E. and Weaver, W. (1949). *The mathematical theory of communication.* Urbana, IL: University of Illinois Press.

Shepard, L. A. (Ed.) (1985). *Encyclopedia of occultism and parapsychology* (Volume Three) (2nd. ed.). Detroit, MI: Gale Research Co.

Shotter, J. D. (1975). *Images of man in psychological research.* London, England: Methuen.

Shotter, J. D. (1984). *Social accountability and selfhood.* Oxford, England: Basil Blackwell.

Shotter, J. D. (1993). Harre, Vygotsky, Bakhtin, Vico, Wittgenstein: Academic discourses and conversational realities. *Journal for the Theory of Social Behaviour, 23*(4), 459-482.

Simpson, C. (1994). *Science of coercion: Communication research and psychological warfare, 1945-1960.* Oxford, England: Oxford University Press.

Simpson, J. A. & Weiner, E. S. C. (1989). *The Oxford English dictionary - Volume XIV* (2nd ed.). Oxford, England: Clarendon Press.

Thayer, L. (1979). Communication: *Sine qua non* of the behavioral sciences. In R. W. Budd and B. D. Ruben (Eds.), *Interdisciplinary approaches to human communication.* Rochelle Park, NJ: Hayden.

Tulving, E. (1972), Episodic and semantic memory. In E. Tulving and W. Donaldson (Eds.), *Organization of memory.* NewYork, NY: Academic Press

Underwood, G. (1978). Concepts in information processing theory. In G. Underwood (Ed.), *Strategies of information processing.* London, England: Academic Press.

Underwood, G. (1982). *Aspects of consciousness: Volume three. Awareness and self-awareness.* London, England: Academic Press.

Underwood, G. (1996). *Implicit cognition.* New York, NY: Oxford University Press.

Waldstein, L. (1926). *The subconscious self and its relation to education and health.* New York, NY: Charles Scribner's Sons. (Original work published 1894)

Weaver, W. (1949). Introductory note on the general setting of the analytical communication studies. In C. E. Shannon and W. Weaver, *The mathematical theory of communication* (pp. 3-28). Urbana, IL: University of Illinois Press.

Weaver, W. (1967). *Science and imagination: Selected papers of Warren Weaver.* New York, NY: Basic Books.

Whyte, L. L. (1978). *The unconscious before Freud.* New York, NY: St Martin's Press. (Original work published 1960)

Wiener, N. (1954). *The human use of human beings: Cybernetics and society* (2nd edition). Garden City, NY: Doubleday Anchor Books.

Williams, R. (1983). *Keywords: A vocabulary of culture and society* (revised edition). London, England: Fontana Press.

Wittgenstein. L. (1953). *Philosophical investigations* (G. E. M. Anscombe, Trans.). Oxford, England: Blackwell Publishers.

Wittgenstein, L. (1958). *The blue and brown books.* New York, NY: Harper Torchbooks.

Wittgenstein, L. (1980). *Remarks on the philosophy of psychology: Volume One* (G. E. M. Anscombe, Trans.). Chicago, IL: University of Chicago Press.

Wundt, W. (1896). *Lectures on human and animal psychology* (2nd ed.) (J. E. Creighton and E. B. Titchener, Trans.). New York, NY: Macmillan. (Original work published 1892)

Index